LETTING GO
into
PERFECT
LOVE

LETTING GO
into
PERFECT
LOVE

Discovering the Extraordinary
After Abuse

Gwendolyn M Plano

SHE WRITES PRESS

Published 2014

Printed in the United States of America

ISBN: 978-1-938314-74-2

Library of Congress Control Number: 2013953911

For information, address:
She Writes Press
1563 Solano Ave #546
Berkeley, CA 94707

To my children, who have accompanied me on
life's amazing journey.

Contents

Introduction

When I was about five years old, standing beneath a tall eucalyptus tree at our desert farm on the outskirts of Brawley, California, I turned to my two younger sisters and said, "Someday we will be big and they will be little," referring to our parents. Though I don't recall the circumstance that evoked this declaration, I do remember my sisters' nods. As we marched off to play, we were confident that this would be the case.

Over the years, I've thought back to this revelatory moment and wondered, *Why did I say that, and what did I mean?* Though I don't have an answer, Mom and Dad did indeed become little with time, their bodies growing tired and their memories slipping from reach. And we became big with responsibilities and caregiving, but was this what I was speaking of as a child of five?

As perplexing as my youthful assertion may seem, there is an undeniable circular quality to life. T. S. Eliot wrote: "What we call the beginning is often the end, and to make an end is to make a beginning." We leave a job and search for a new one; we end a relationship and begin another; and we say our earthly good-byes to a beloved friend or family member and welcome a newborn. Our beginnings and endings blur as they repeat through one experience after another.

Haven't we all been told that when one door closes, another

opens? We may protest the platitude as we condemn the injustice, the indignity, the tragedy of our situation—whatever it may be. Our hearts may break because of the sorrow we know; our bodies may collapse beneath the pain we endure. Hope may elude us as love withers, but with time, the door of hope opens and we acquiesce to possibility.

It is about this ebb and flow of the human journey that I write.

We learn about life through family interactions, significant events, and stories passed down through generations. Our families are melting pots of behavioral and physical attributes. As impressionable children, we adopt and assimilate these characteristics as our own, and thus we are told, "You are just like your father [or mother or aunt or uncle]," because we have innocently learned their script.

My father lived through the Great Depression, and that ordeal left an indelible imprint on him. He expected much of us and had no patience for halfhearted efforts. I grew up hearing accounts of survival, of hardships faced and surmounted. In contrast, my mother knew deep sadness. She lost her mother at a very early age and suffered that loss throughout her life. Her stories were of selflessness, penance, and sacrifice. Together my parents taught me about the great expanse of human struggle, and imperceptibly their words found a place in my heart—until the stories became my own.

Because these family patterns become part of us as impressionable children, we imagine everyone shares the same vantage point, but such is not the case. We each have a different social history that influences how we perceive and respond to life. A challenge for me may be an opportunity for you. It depends upon the lens through which we see.

Still, common ideals beckon all of us. When we are at weddings and witness lovers commit to each other, their passion triggers our own. When we watch the sun set over the ocean or mountains high, such splendor makes our hearts soar. When we feel the excitement of a musical composition or the hug of an innocent child, we are lifted beyond ourselves into bliss. And after our minds have quieted and our bodies become still, we rest in the timelessness of serenity. Joy and peace summon all of us, irrespective of our differences. But the most elusive value, the one that encompasses all others and the one that propels us most, is love.

Our family histories, our places of worship, and society in general inform us about these ideals. We trek through life looking for and trying to generate the standard we've been taught exists: unconditional love, ecstatic joy, and pervasive peace. Our intentions are virtuous, but more often than not, we fall short of our desired goal and then try to create the illusion of that which we seek. It is our created illusions that lead to secrets and untold torments. We want to believe that we have what we don't have, and we want others to think that we have found and are living our bliss.

The pages of this book invite you into my life journey, replete with childhood stories and adult meanderings. You will read of my search for love, joy, and peace and will note the ways in which I tried to preserve the illusion of these ideals when I could not find that which I sought. I encourage you to listen to your heart as you travel with me. You may come to understand yourself a little differently, because the pursuit of these fundamental elements of life is a widespread quest. As you accompany me, you may also realize that your family has secrets just as my family did, and when you unravel those hidden parts of your experience, you may discover that they originated to protect both your family and the facade of achievement.

Though the state of affairs surrounding my story may be quite different from yours, I suspect you will find much of it familiar. Our joys and our heartaches are, curiously, both unique and universal. Through either sentiment, we communicate with and understand one another. The details of my life travels are as consequential as the details of yours, because we walk a shared path.

When I was a young child, countrywomen gathered to sew quilts for celebrations and passings. Mother took us with her when she met with her friends in the basement of the rural Methodist church, beside the dirt road at the edge of the sugar beet fields. We were told to play quietly with our coloring books while they worked. Sometimes we did; other times we did not and chose instead to run wild through the church.

The women stacked their scraps of cloth next to the folded yards of batting on the table near the wall. I saw my dresses there—pieces of them—and wondered about the other striped and flowered samples of fabric. To whom did these fragments belong?

Sometimes I snuck under the stretched material on the large wooden frame and listened as the women stitched and knotted. They talked about their families, about local people, about their hardships, and about love. When they cried, I cried—even if I did not quite understand. It was their emotion that spoke to me. Later I would ask Mom about what I had heard, but she always said it was *private*, not something for me to know. I was left with just strands of stories—and feelings.

"He grabbed me around the neck," Bonnie said. "I can't even wear my pearls now, can't have anything around my neck." *Why not?* I thought from my hiding place near her feet. As the women consoled her, I was left with questions—and fear. Who did this, and why?

"Mary lost her baby earlier this week. It wasn't full-term. She got to hold it, though," Dorothy explained. "When I lost mine, they took it away," she said tearfully. Mom whispered something in return, and I strained to hear—something about another baby lost before its time. I desperately wanted to know more, but I never did, until many years later.

"Did you hear about Jane's husband? Cut his arm on the blade of the plow and hasn't been able to work since. Awful, awful," Patty said.

"Do you suppose we could bring over dinner?" Mom replied.

The women quickly agreed and then decided to alternate nights among them. I thought about Theresa and wondered if she was okay. Her daddy was hurt, and that made me sad. Was there something I should do too?

I learned a lot through the stories these countrywomen shared. Their cloth leftovers rhythmically sewn one to another helped me see the interconnectedness of life—though at the time, I understood only that the collected and fastened snippets created something beautiful for a family in need or for newlyweds just starting their life together.

This book is a quilt of sorts, a patchwork of stories each with its own sorrows and joys, connected by and resulting in a life that is mine. I've attempted to capture events that helped shape the person I am now by rereading old journals, as well as reports from doctors, attorneys, and counselors. Though the stories are linked chronologically, they sometimes span years and interweave with other events. I've changed the names of my family members and associates because the book is not about them; it is about my journey, and ultimately the twists and turns of life that bring all of us home to ourselves.

While walking our life path, I think, very few of us would choose the obstacles presented to us. It is only later, after the storms have passed and the rains lifted, that we see (sometimes dimly) the blessings in our fate. We do not need to condone the circumstances to recognize the steps we have taken toward wholeness through the quandaries of our destiny. But honoring our courage, resilience, and love opens the once-closed door to the extraordinary.

One such difficulty for me was a physically and emotionally abusive marriage of twenty-five years. I tried in all the ways I could to fashion the model family of which I had dreamed, even in the face of distressing impediments. But I was steadfast. I accepted my predicament because I didn't know what to do. As the chapters to follow will reveal, over time I became less and less capable of choice. I was captive to dreams and to fear—until grace awakened me.

My hope is that in my responses to my experiences, you will recognize yourself, even though you may not have known the same difficulties. Perhaps you denied your truth in another way, thinking that you, too, were supporting a higher good.

A central component of my journey involves my children, three sons and one daughter. They are an integral part of my life story, and throughout these chapters, they travel alongside me as I wrestle with decisions that involve them.

Like mothers everywhere, I marveled at each child's birth. During those first precious moments, while doctors, midwives, nurses, and staff were busy with the birth details, I fell in love with my newborn. I would softly rub my baby's sweet head, stare into his or her sleepy eyes, and count perfect little fingers and toes. I was overcome by love, and my tears flowed. My pervasive desire at the time was very elementary: I wanted only to protect my treasured gift.

Most parents, and in particular mothers, feel unconditional love at the birth of their child. It is perhaps a human being's first glimpse of Perfect Love. Our labor may have been lengthy, the conditions of our life may have been complicated, but all such matters fade in the light of the beautiful child we behold. We are not worried about the baby's prospective career; we don't think about what schools the baby will attend. We are not even concerned about our own personal troubles—financial or otherwise. We simply want what is best for our child. Because of this fervent desire, a mother's soul is wounded if her child is harmed.

When my daughter recalled being molested by two priests and a nun, she was thrown into an abyss of despair—and I with her. The horror of what she endured sent shock waves throughout our entire family, and my devastation was overwhelming. There is no greater sorrow for a mother than to see her child in pain. I would gladly have suffered in my daughter's stead. As you read the chapter with this testimony, my hope is that you will pay homage to the anguish you have endured and see anew our collective, hallowed journey.

Mothers know what is expected of them. The television families of the fifties, sixties, and seventies—captured on such shows as *The Adventures of Ozzie and Harriet*, *Father Knows Best*, and *The Brady Bunch*—may have faded from our memories, but they have not vanished in our collective consciousness. Though times have changed, the composite image of the perfect family persists, and it is this ideal that we mothers try to replicate in our homes. Because of our heartfelt aspiration to provide only the best for our sons and daughters, we sometimes confuse what is real with what is imaginary. We may even opt for the dream and hide what does not correspond with the fantasy. Consciously or unconsciously, we decide to provide our children with what we had *and* what we think we did not have as children but wanted.

Most of us live with expectations that colleagues or friends or our communities place on us, but mothers carry a particular burden. We are measured by prior and future generations, by societal norms, and by other mothers.

"My in-laws are visiting this Wednesday," I told my neighbor Barbara one day. "I should paint the hallway before they arrive. The kids have drawn stick figures on the walls."

"I don't know about your mother-in-law, but I always check the baseboards in a house," Barbara replied. "If there is dust, then I know that the person who lives there has not cleaned as she should—no matter what her home looks like."

When Barbara told me this, I shuddered as I thought about my baseboards. *Have I ever cleaned them?* I thought. I tried to keep things tidy, but between my full-time work and family responsibilities, I had barely a minute on my own.

"Goodness, I have a lot to do over the next few days," I moaned.

"Well, if you need help, give me a call," Barbara responded generously.

"Thank you," I replied, but inside I was thinking, *Never! What would she find besides dirty baseboards?*

Mothers live with these types of imposed expectations. So when our child does not sell all his class candy, it is we who are at fault. If our child neglects his homework or acts up, it is we whom the school contacts.

"Your son threw his backpack down the stairwell, Mrs. Taylor," the middle-school principal said when I answered the phone one day. "He could have hurt someone."

"I'm so sorry," I quickly responded. "I'll talk with him as soon as he gets home."

"You need to pick him up now. We're suspending him for the week. We can't have this kind of behavior," the principal continued.

"It will take me a few minutes to get there," I replied. "I need to explain this to my boss."

"He'll be waiting for you in my office. And by the way, I know I can expect your support on this. We must have a united front!" he tersely concluded.

Without my knowing the full story of this transgression, the principal expected a certain response from me, and his tone of voice communicated that he was as frustrated with me, the mother of this young criminal in the making, as he was with my son. I had to wonder, would he have responded similarly to my husband?

We are all guided by life challenges and blessings. Much like directional signs, these hurdles and affirmations provide us with the opportunity to reconsider, to reevaluate, and to choose our way yet again. Most of our choices are mundane, but some are chillingly difficult, and sometimes our unique life prism distorts the situation before us in such a way that we do not see the obvious. As the chapters that follow will reveal, at times I was blind to what others could plainly see.

To go back through the pages of time to write this book has been an unexpected healing adventure. As I connected my early experiences to the decisions that followed, I saw that I helped create my stories. I was not a hapless victim; rather, I was a participant. Sometimes my choices were courageous and righteous; other times, they were driven by fear and shame. As I realized my participation in some of the tumultuous events of my life, the unanticipated occurred—I began to let go of judgment, and as I did so, forgiveness emerged. Instead of chastising myself for my failings, I felt profound tenderness and respect for the person I was so many years ago. These sentiments extended beyond just me, for as I accepted myself, I accepted others as well. We all do the best we can with the decisions before us, but none of us is perfect. What is astounding is that no matter where we are in life and no matter what we are facing at the time, we can always choose a different path that can lead us to the joy we seek.

Through the process of writing this book, I realized how I was deeply supported and loved throughout my life. It was a delusion to imagine that I was alone, just as it was to imagine that I was unworthy of love. When tragedy is part of our life, it consumes us. Its coldness is deep-seated, and it can entrap our hearts, our hopes, and our dreams. We can lose perspective, and in such a state, no words can comfort us. It is only as we look back, sometimes years later, that we regain perspective—and possibly find a deeper meaning if we have changed for the better because of what we have withstood.

When my father's mother came to live with us, my dad purchased a mobile home for her and situated it a few yards from our house. Grandma spent her time there, quietly embroidering and stitching intricate quilts. She used the leftover scraps of cloth from my sisters' and my sewing projects. From these simple pieces, she generated beautiful spreads for the entire family. After drawing a design, she would cut the fabric into squares, triangles, and diamonds. Then she'd sit and stitch, rocking slowly to and fro. When I sat with her, she told me about growing up in Georgia, about her father, who was a preacher and a farmer, and about her siblings. She told me she learned to read by studying a dictionary and said she always had a knack for playing the piano. Her stories were of times long past, sometimes funny and sometimes sad, and as she spoke I could see the tales were alive in the present; they filled her world when she stitched.

"I'm going to tell you what happened to me in a buggy," she said one day as I watched her sew. "You know what a buggy is?" I nodded that I did. I had seen them on television.

"Well, I had a boyfriend, and he picked me up in his buggy. We were going to an all-day singing at church. And I guess my friend ran out of dry feed for his horse. Anyway, we were about halfway to the singing when the horse had to use the bathroom. I wore a white dress. Oh, what a mess I was in. My dress was more green than white! My face became burnt red, and I cried and told my friend I wanted to go home. I fell on the bed and cried more. Then, around noon, a man called and said they wanted me to play the piano that eve. So he sent for me, and then I felt better. I hope you never go through this," she said with a smile.

I was confident that I would never encounter the same, but when I was in high school, my sister and I were driving to town in our family's old Pontiac station wagon. We heard a loud *thump-thump*, and the car swerved side to side. I pulled off the road and noticed a flat tire. Neither of us had ever changed a tire, but for the next several hours, we labored to do so. When we finished, our clothes weren't green like Grandma's, but they were black from the tire and covered with dirt. A man drove by just as we were finishing and tried not to laugh.

"Well, I'll be! I've never seen anything like it," he said. "I didn't know it was possible."

"What are you talking about?" I said, becoming frustrated by his amusement.

"You've put the tire on backwards," he laughed.

"What? I didn't know there was a front or back to a tire," I said.

"You can make it to town," he added. "But you'd better go to the filling station and have them put it on right. Don't try to drive farther on it as it is," he warned, still chuckling.

"Okay," I responded, thinking anything but kind thoughts.

I never got to tell Grandma this story, but I think she would have been amused. It wasn't as dramatic as hers, but much about it was the same.

My most beloved quilt was a patchwork of a star radiating to the four corners of the comforter. This giant mandala of color had life sewn into it: my lilac polka-dotted Easter dress, my sister's flowered apron that earned her a blue ribbon at the fair, my mother's seersucker blouse—all were there, the remnants of cloth that we no longer needed. When I finger the fabric pieces, some soft, some crisp, I see my grandma—her hands stiffened and her eyes dim with age. I hear again her stories of sorrows and joys, and I see my own. This quilt, more than the others, pulses with the beginnings and endings of life.

I don't sew like I did as a child. My writing has become my stretched cloth; it is the medium for my stories. Just as I unfold my grandma's quilt and allow my eyes to wander through the maze of colors and print designs, reliving the tales now long gone, I invite you to do the same with this book.

I recently purchased a canvas print by the artist Clare Goodwin, of a mandala entitled *Soul's Stillness*. This beautiful artwork draws one into the center, where light emanates. As lovely as a stained-glass window, the mandala reaches beyond time and speaks to heart reality. Clare quotes John O'Donohue in explaining her work: "When your way of belonging in the world is truthful to your nature and your dreams, your heart finds contentment and your soul finds stillness. You are able to participate fully in the joy and adventure of exploration, and your life opens up for living joyfully, powerfully, and tenderly."

Sometimes it takes a lifetime to find such stillness and freedom. *Letting Go into Perfect Love* is about that journey.

The Beginning

I am a farmer's daughter, the firstborn of nine. I grew up to the sounds of roosters crowing and crickets chirping. They were as much a part of my life as hard work and sacrifice. When my mother was sick or having babies, I was in charge of the little ones, making sure their needs were met and the chores completed. Before I could read, I prepared the meals and baked the pies. I'd push a chair to the kitchen countertop so that I could reach the dishes and the stove. Life was simple on the farm: if there was a problem, you fixed it, no matter what your age might be.

Mom was born and raised in Imperial Valley, the southernmost area of California, and that is where I grew up as well. Her father was considered a pioneer to the region, because his family had migrated from Iowa in the early 1900s to farm the desert wasteland. He came from a family of Methodist preachers and farmers. Through friends he met his future wife, a lighthearted Irish Catholic woman who captivated him from the moment they met. They laughed about their religious differences, married quickly, and settled about eight miles outside the small town of Brawley. By all accounts, they were a happy couple, and they had five children together; my mother was one of the first identical twins born in the area. Then the unthinkable happened.

"Your grandmother was on her way to pick us up at school,"

Mom recounted. "There were no stop signs on the roads back then, and her car was broadsided by a truck going through the intersection at the same time as she." When my mother told us this story, she cried. A few times she mentioned that maybe she was to blame, because she had asked her mother not to be late. "If only she hadn't rushed…"

"Your grandmother did not die immediately; she lived a few hours in the hospital," she told us. "She was pregnant, and the baby died instantly from the impact. My baby sister was also in the car; she was hurt but did not have to be hospitalized. It was so, so sad," she said tearfully, her voice trailing off. Mom was eight when her mother died.

After the accident, the five children went to live with their aunt and uncle. Their father needed time to mourn and couldn't care for the children and work at the same time. More than a year later, he was introduced to a single mother who was cleaning homes in the area. They fell in love and married soon afterward. My mother and her siblings went back home with their father—and their new stepmother and stepsister. Within a couple of years, they welcomed another sister to the family, and then there were seven children.

Mom and her siblings felt the sorrow of their mother's passing throughout their lives, and after their father remarried, they felt bereft of both of their parents' love.

"When my father remarried, I felt like we were in the way," my mom's sister reminisced. "It was no one's fault," she added. "It just wasn't the same as before. Your grandfather had always sung the old Stephen Foster songs with us: 'Home on the Range,' 'Beautiful Dreamer,' and 'Oh! Susanna.' He'd tuck us into our beds on the screened porch, and we'd sing until we fell asleep. But when he married again, he didn't sing to us anymore.

"Don't get me wrong," she explained, "we loved our new sisters, but it was not the same as before."

By country standards, my mother's father was successful. He owned farmland and had livestock. He was active in the community—serving as a sheriff and otherwise participating in the Elks Club and various farm organizations. Respected for his generosity and wisdom, people turned to him for help. And, when he wasn't working in the fields or playing with his children, he enjoyed a game of golf.

When World War II was declared, my mother wanted to do her part. Rosie the Riveter signs posted at the high school read WE CAN DO IT! My mother wanted to work on airplanes just like Rosie. When she graduated from high school, she got her parents' permission to go to San Diego to work at the Convair Consolidated Aircraft plant. Her stepmother's sister had a boardinghouse nearby where she could stay. Her job, like the fictional Rosie the Riveter's, was to fasten pieces of metal together. That is where Mom and Dad met.

Unlike my mother, my father had a difficult childhood. He was born in the rolling hills of Carter, Oklahoma, and spent most of his youth in and around that area and parts of northwestern Arkansas. His family knew the worst of poverty and the Dust Bowl.

"We could see it coming, dark and threatening like a storm, but it was sand and dirt," Dad explained to us. "We thought we were high society because we lived in two tents—some families had only one. We slept in one tent and had three mattresses for the nine of us; the other tent was smaller, and we used it for cooking. There was no flooring, just sand. When the winds came, we ran to a dugout where your grandma kept potatoes and turnips. We could hardly breathe, but it was better inside than outside. Everything was covered with dirt and sand."

My father grew up in an itinerant family. They moved twenty-seven times when he was a youngster, to wherever my grandfather could find work. They'd pack up the tents and load their sparse belongings onto an old truck and head to the next location. They had no electricity, no plumbing, and no outhouse.

"Your grandpa would look for a flat space for the tents and then tell us to start digging the well. We didn't much like doing that, but we had no choice. We had to have water!" my father would explain.

"We'd lower a bucket into the hole to get water. That's what we'd drink."

Because of this instability, my father finished about eight years of school. He was needed in the cotton fields, and it was there that his mother went into labor with twins. They tried to get help for her, my father explained to us, but the babies arrived before it came. The tiny infants struggled for life, but such was not to be their fate.

"You kids have it lucky," he reminded us. "We were dirt-poor when I was your age; the dust took everything from us. Sometimes we had no food, but your grandma did the best she could, making cornbread with water and lard.

"I would go out in the morning, looking for rabbits," he said, "and it was a *good* day when I brought one home. I swore that when I grew up and had kids, they'd never go hungry." Dad's eyes watered a bit when he reminded us of this. "You may not have much, but you have food, and that is more than what I could expect as a child!"

He told us story after story of survival, of doing all that he could to earn a few pennies to help the family: he cleaned chicken coops and pigsties, plowed the fields, harvested wheat, pitched hay, cut wood, helped build or move outhouses. They were starving and desperate, and any work was good work.

When Dad told us these stories, we felt anxious gratitude. There was always the sense that such travails could befall us at any time, and we had to be prepared for the worst. We understood that we had to work hard, lest we be impoverished as well. "*Never* make fun of someone who has less than you," he warned. "You might be that person someday."

Even after decades had passed, the Great Depression lived in my father. It was as much a part of his life as the air he breathed. His formative years were shaped by the harshest adversity.

At seventeen years old, Dad joined the Civilian Conservation Corps and stayed for two terms. He earned $30 per month, of which $22 went to his parents. This was more money than he or his family had ever seen. He learned about erosion control and learned to survey land; both skills proved helpful later in life. When the war started, he joined the Navy.

Dad was an excellent marksman—a talent he learned when he was just a child—and he was an excellent metalsmith. The Navy wanted him to teach riflery, but the need for skilled metalsmiths was greater, so the Navy released him to work at Convair Consolidated in San Diego.

"When I saw your mom on the wing of a B-24 bomber, I knew that she was the one for me," he reminisced. "She wore a purple sweater the first time I saw her; I had never seen anyone so pretty. My buddy was next to me, and I turned to him and said, 'She's the one for me!'" Mom always giggled when Dad told us this story.

My mother and father married in 1946 and moved to Imperial Valley, where my father worked for my grandfather on his farm. I was the first of their five daughters and four sons.

For much of my early years, we lived in the same farmhouse that my mother grew up in. The three older girls slept on a bed in the attic underneath the slanted ceilings. We'd alternate who got to sleep on the side of the bed and who got the middle. Often we'd climb up the stairs to our attic escape to see the rocker swaying to and fro; it had been our grandmother's chair, and even though we had never met her, we knew that she was with us.

My mother was a devout Catholic, and my father was raised Church of Christ. Sometimes the mix of religious beliefs provoked discussions that left my siblings and me confused about what was true and what was not. Even so, both parents were strict about prayers, and my father ultimately deferred to my mother about any-thing religious. He had promised when he married my mother to raise his children Catholic, and that was a promise he kept.

Mother prayed throughout the day. When she washed dishes, folded clothes, walked from one room to another, she said the rosary or some other prayer. Her barely audible supplications were a reminder to all of us that there was another realm to life. When we hurt ourselves playing or became ill, Mom would say, "Make your suffering worth something. Offer it up for the poor souls in purgatory." As children, we weren't quite sure what this meant, but we knew that purgatory was not a happy place. It was neither heaven nor hell; it was the in-between world where souls waited for someone to set them free through prayers. In this mix of religiosity, I acquired the notion that pain could be redemptive, that it was a way to become a better person.

Every Sunday, Mother drove us to Mass in Brawley. We children would crowd into the car and push and shove until we found our space. When I was six years old, something dreadful occurred. Mom drove us home from church, and as she got to the driveway of our farmhouse, a worker ran to the car.

"There was a terrible accident, terrible!" He panted. "Your husband is at the hospital."

"Is he okay?" Mom shouted with an eerie urgency.

"He's lost his arm, but he's okay," he said, his eyes wide with fright.

We never got out of the car that morning. Mom simply turned the car around quickly and headed back to town. No one spoke as she rushed to the hospital; we saw her fear and felt it ourselves. I turned and looked at my younger siblings; they were scared like I was. My five- and four-year-old sisters and two- and one-year-old brothers stared at me, not knowing what had happened. "We'll be okay," I whispered, as I held my youngest brother, who was whimpering.

Later we learned that our father was cleaning the rollers of a combine when his glove got caught, and his arm was pulled into the revolving blades. There was a farmworker nearby, and my father yelled for help. He asked the man to cut off his arm, because there was no other way to get his arm out of the mechanism. The worker refused to do so, but he handed my father the ax. The choice was a dreary one: bleed to death or cut off his own arm. He chose the latter.

"Things are going to be different," Mom later explained to us. "Your dad won't be able to do many of the things he's done in the past."

"But what will Dad do?" I inquired tearfully.

"He will just have to get another arm—like a dolly's arm," Mom responded, trying to calm my fears.

I thought about my dolls—a Raggedy Ann doll my grandmother had made and a plastic doll that Santa had left. *Their arms went up and down if I moved them, but how would Dad's arm move? I wondered.*

When Dad came home from the hospital, he sat near a window staring into the distance. His arm was covered with bandages, and he kept it propped up with pillows. We children were accustomed to climbing onto his lap to cuddle and play, but now we were told repeatedly, *Do not touch the arm.* Dad was in a lot of pain.

Local farmers came by to see my father and brought a television as a gift. It was our first, and we were entranced. Dad watched the shows, but it was as though he were not there. I tried to get his attention, asking if he would like some water or something to eat, but usually he said nothing. It seemed he was in another world.

For a ruggedly independent man who needed his hands for his work, the accident was a serious misfortune. What I didn't realize at the time was that my father was deciding his next course of action. He was determined to surmount even a missing arm. When the stub healed, he got an artificial arm with a hook that helped him hold and move things. It wasn't quite the "dolly's arm" that I had imagined, but it helped. Still, the hook was not a hand, and he required our assistance at times.

"Gwen," Dad would call, "come here and hold the nail." I would shudder when he called me, because I was frightened of being hurt. He'd position the long spike on the thick wood, and I would hold it there while he swung the sledgehammer over his head to slam the nail. He never missed, but I feared he would, and my arm would tremble.

"Hold still!" Dad would insist. And I would try to be still.

Dad was never one to complain, but after the accident, he would not tolerate our disgruntlements. "If you have a problem," he'd say firmly, "find a solution. Whining never did anyone any good." My father did not speak about the accident or his pain, but we knew the latter based on the level of his frustration. He kept his miseries to himself, and he expected us to do the same.

Our lives changed after Dad lost his arm. Some of the laughter in the house disappeared. Dad didn't play with us in the same ways in which he had in the past. He couldn't throw us in the air or swing us around in a circle; he couldn't make his jumping handkerchief-mouse that would amuse us on hot summer nights. He couldn't milk the cows or cut his own meat at the dinner table. And what he couldn't do greatly aggravated him. He hated limitations, and this hate fueled his resolve. He was determined to do with one arm what many could not do with two.

My father did battle with his handicap, and our family was part of that battle. At times he was brusque with our mother and with us, and when he wanted something done, he wanted it done immediately. His impatience sometimes got the best of him.

"Gwen, come in here!" he demanded one day. He thought I had done something that I had not. "What were you doing? You're not to go into my truck!"

I tried to explain that I hadn't done anything, but my responses made him angrier, and he kicked me. I ran into the bathroom crying and locked the door; Mother came after me.

"Open the door, Gwen, open the door!" she insisted. I grudgingly complied, still crying.

"Dad is working so hard, sometimes he just can't help himself," she said, but her statement fell on deaf ears. I felt crushed by the injustice.

"He loves you very much, Gwen. Don't you know that? You are the one he played with the most," Mom said pleadingly. I was surprised by her comment, because I thought that no one loved me—I was the oldest, the one who was counted on to handle everything. While my younger siblings were cuddled and cared for, I sat by myself hungry for the same affection.

"But I didn't do it, Mom," I said through my tears.

"I know, I know. He's sorry, Gwen; he just can't tell you that right now," she explained.

My younger siblings did not know the father I knew before the accident. They knew only the impatient man who required much of them. I knew of a different father, one who carved figurines from squares of wood, who played the harmonica in the evenings for our amusement, who comforted babies on his shoulder, patting them to sleep. My siblings were not old enough to remember life when our father had two arms, but I could remember, and those memories helped me look beyond his at times volatile disposition.

My parents taught us to face our challenges head-on and find a way to overcome the difficulty. When swarms of crickets closed the highway by our home and brought night to the day, Dad had us shut all the windows, doors, and vents and stay in the house. The insects got into the attic and the crawlspace, but only a few made it into our living area. This unprecedented plague of biblical proportions became a way for Dad to teach us about managing difficulties.

"When you are confronted with a problem, figure out what you can do to make things better," he said. "You may not be able to solve the problem, but doing something is better than doing nothing at all."

We were a busy household of ordered chaos. The boys had their responsibilities; the girls had theirs. We got up at the break of dawn and went to bed just after dusk. When we got back from school, we did our homework; only after this could we play. Much was expected of us because our father expected much of himself. If we did not "give our all," we soon regretted our halfheartedness, because Dad would make us do the task again—and again—until we did it right.

As children we did not have money, and I wanted to earn some.

When I was around seven or eight years of age, there wasn't much I could do, but I was willing to try most anything.

"Dad, can I earn some money?" I asked.

"Sure," he immediately responded. "You see the workers in that field?" he said, pointing to the cotton pickers.

"Yes, I see them," I replied.

"Do you want to work with them?" he asked, and I nodded yes.

"Okay, let's get you a bag. When you fill it, a man will weigh it and you'll get paid by the pound," he explained. I was elated, but my sentiment was short-lived.

The pickers were more than a little amused by my attempts to pull the cotton from its casing, but, seeing my distress, a kind lady stopped and showed me how to take the cotton from the boll without pricking my fingers on the needle-sharp edges. Like the workers, I dragged the big cloth bag behind me as I gathered the cotton from the plants. After a few hours, my bag was barely full, while my picking comrades had filled theirs. On that hot summer day, I learned that earning money meant hard work. When I eventually got paid, I fingered my coins as though they were gold.

Dad was quite resourceful. He wanted to return to the South to see his family, but he couldn't fit all of us into the car. To solve the problem, he bought an old bus and removed all the seats on one side, replacing them with bunk beds. He then created a camping kitchen in the back of the bus. With these changes, our whole family was able to travel together economically. "Where there's a will, there's a way," Dad would say to us. And we knew it to be true, because he proved it time and time again.

When we visited our Southern relatives, we were the "Catholic kids" among our Protestant cousins. This meant nothing to us, except that occasionally we heard comments about who was saved and who was not. With parents from different religious backgrounds, we had grown up accepting the fact that there were a variety of ways to worship God. Nevertheless, we felt like outsiders. It was the food that drew us in, especially the desserts: sweet-potato pie and coconut-topped oatmeal cake. We hadn't tasted anything so delectable.

As we passed through one state after another, we saw things that we had never seen before—bathrooms marked WHITES ONLY, and diners with segregated areas. I asked Mom about this.

"Mom, did you see that sign over there, 'Whites Only'? What does that mean?" I asked.

"It's complicated, Gwen. Keep in mind that there are always two sides to a story," she replied.

"But what does it mean?" I persisted.

"Well, there are hard feelings in some areas of the South between people with white skin and people with dark skin. So they handle those feelings by separating the two groups," she explained.

I thought this very odd, because I envied the beautiful dark skin of my classmates in the country school I attended. Most of them were Mexican; some were the daughters of migrants who cut the sugarcane or picked cotton near our home. While they could run freely in the sun, I had to cover my freckled white skin because I sunburned easily. I couldn't imagine being upset with them because of their skin color. They were my friends.

I was sickly as a child, struggling with asthma, especially during the summer harvest. From my earliest years, I accompanied my grandmother Mamo to San Diego when the alfalfa was cut. The pollen from the fresh-cut grasses closed my lungs and left me gasping. Mamo was my rescuer, taking me to her summer home by the beach.

San Diego became my childhood sanctuary. I dreamed of eventually moving there, for it was the epitome of all things wonderful. I went with Mamo to the theater, to large shopping malls, to movies, to restaurants, and to the beaches. Though I felt quite awkward in my hand-me-down clothes and worn-out shoes, I nevertheless dreamed of sometime in the future when I would have nicer clothes and better shoes and perhaps a sense of belonging. I missed my family, of course, but I was excited to be where I could breathe and where I could explore new things.

Every evening, Mamo reminded me to say my prayers. One night I innocently shared what I was saying.

"I'm praying to suffer a lot before I die, so that I won't go to purgatory," I said with a bit of pride.

"Gwen, that is a terrible prayer!" Mamo responded quickly and with horror in her voice. "You should never ask for such things. Pray instead to have good health and a long life. That is what I do," she said firmly.

"Okay," I responded timidly, but I was torn. Some of the first books that I read were about the saints, and without exception, their lives were marked by suffering. I read of Father Damien in Molokai, working among the lepers, and how he died with them. I read about Saint Francis and Saint Clare of Assisi, and their health travails. I read about Saint Bernadette and identified with her chronic asthma and other medical problems. All the saints suffered notably and sometimes sought out more suffering as their penance. As an impressionable young girl, I thought they were the role models to follow, but Mamo's reaction left me wondering. *Maybe it's just Methodists who think that way*, I concluded.

I didn't tell her about walking barefoot on the parched dirt road by our house on a sweltering summer day. For more than a week afterward, I grappled with bandages to cover the blisters I got from this venture. I thought my pain was somehow blessed, but now I questioned if that was true. Was Mamo right?

When I was nine years old, Mother arranged for my siblings and me to attend the Catholic school in Brawley. We had to ride the high school bus to get to school. We were the strange little kids among a much older group of adolescents. Sometimes we were taunted, but most of the time we coexisted. We'd walk three-quarters of a mile from the high school to our school and return by the same route. When we actually started high school, we already knew our bus and the rural roads it traveled.

The Catholic school was very different from the country school I had attended. We were taught about sin and eternal punishment; we studied the biblical stories and the lives of the saints; and we learned what it meant to be a Catholic. Though none of this seemed to bother the other students, all the dos and don'ts made me anxious. I worried if I was doing everything right. In contrast, my memories of the country school were lighthearted and included recollections of learning musical rhythm and dance steps, watercolor painting and geography.

In high school, I alternated between wanting to be a teacher and wanting to be a doctor. To be either, I needed to go to college, which meant convincing my father. He did not believe there was any value for a girl to go to college, because "she will just get married," he'd say to my mother. Dad and Mom argued this point many times. Finally, my mother reminded him that she had always wanted to go to college even *after* she was married. "The girls deserve this opportunity as much as the boys," she insisted, and eventually Dad conceded. I would be able to go to the local community college, and if I did well, I could transfer to a university.

Dad bought an old two-door Cadillac from a friend so that I could commute to the community college in the Valley. Between classes and after chores in the evenings, I studied and finished the year with high grades—and an acceptance letter from a university in San Francisco. Dad was pleased with my success, though he was apprehensive about my attending a college so far away from the farm.

"Are you sure this is what you want, Gwen?" he asked cautiously.

"I am, Dad. I am ready now," I said.

He simply responded, "Okay. Let's do it."

Fields of alfalfa, cotton, and sugar beets stretched in all directions from our crowded home in the hot Southern California desert, but my dreams lay beyond that expanse. As much as I loved the simple beauty of desert wildflowers and the white sand dunes behind our home, I longed for the city and the adventure it might bring.

The Visitation

With a tattered suitcase packed with my few belongings, I boarded a Greyhound bus for San Francisco. Over the next twelve hours or so, deserts and mountains, the ocean and the forests sped by my window. I watched as passengers climbed on and then off the bus, until finally I glimpsed the city through the twilight shadows. It pulsed with light, and my excitement screamed for attention. Moving from a farm to a city is more than just a trip; it is a life-altering experience.

Walking into the residence I shared with three other female students at the university was surreal. I had just traveled six hundred miles or more, and though I was in the middle of a grand metropolis, in my heart I was still on the farm. My T-shirt and jeans betrayed me as surely as my naïveté as I stared at my roommates, who looked like models from the magazines in grocery stores. They were beautiful and perfect, and they had a lot of clothes. They filled the closet with dresses for all occasions and stacked their shoes neatly just beneath the gowns. I had never seen such a rainbow of footwear. I had brought all the shoes I owned—my *good* pair and my *old* pair— and as I faced our shared walk-in closet, I wondered if I belonged there and if my dream was realistic.

Though I felt conspicuously out of place, I loved the area. The city was vibrant, and the university was beautiful. Golden Gate Park was just across the street, and that is where I met Bruce. I was walking along the periphery of the park when he approached.

"Hey, do you go to USF?" he said enthusiastically.

"Yes," I responded cautiously, wondering if I should say anything at all.

"I thought I saw you in the hallway. I'm a student too. My name is Bruce; what's yours?"

My shyness did not deter him. As he walked alongside me, he talked nonstop about how he wanted to write the next best seller, how he loved music, how he liked to travel. By the time we returned to campus, it felt as if we had known each other for months. Bruce's outgoing personality balanced my introspective nature. Over the academic year, we walked much of the city, attended outdoor concerts in the park, explored nearby towns, and just had fun. He was always ready to try something new, and his boldness was contagious. At the end of the year, however, we had to say good-bye. I needed to transfer to a public university closer to home where costs would be much more reasonable.

Bruce and I stayed in touch through letters and random phone calls. He also traveled to see me whenever he could. I was enrolled in a university in San Diego, which was midway between his family and my family. During school breaks, we visited with our families, and otherwise enjoyed the beaches, went to performances at the Old Globe Theatre, and just spent time with each other. Then, on a beautiful Sunday afternoon, Bruce got down on one knee and asked me to marry him.

"I don't have much," he explained as he presented me with an engagement ring, "but you are everything to me. You are the most beautiful woman I have ever met." In his characteristic style, he added, "Let's not worry about details. It will be okay."

I was elated and quickly said yes. At twenty years of age, most of my friends were already married. I did not want to be the last one. Besides, when I was with Bruce, I was happy. He'd wrap his arms around my waist and swing me high in the air. "You're my sweetheart," he'd say. If there is such a thing as puppy love, surely I felt it then.

Bruce and I saw each other limitedly during the academic year, and most of our time together was focused on the upcoming nuptials. As the date neared, however, Bruce shared some alarming stories. He talked about people chasing him; he mentioned his mother trying to poison him; he questioned whether he was actually a woman in a man's body. He grew increasingly restless and afraid. Just before the wedding, his behavior radically changed.

Bruce had a part-time job loading Coca-Cola trucks at a nearby distribution center, and one evening he returned from work terrified.

"Men with machine guns surrounded the building and held us at gunpoint," he said. "They are Mafia, and they wanted cash. I confronted them, but...but...they said they'd take me out if I said another word!" He panted.

"Where was Charlie?" I asked, referring to his coworker.

"Charlie? He's one of them!" Bruce said. "Can't trust anyone! The place is crawlin' with commies and criminals."

I knew Charlie; he was a kind family man, definitely not a Mafioso. As we talked, Bruce looked wildly around the room and ran into the bedroom. "They're here," he shouted. "Quick, hide!" I could see no one, and in that moment, I realized that Bruce was hallucinating. Hiding under the bed, he screamed into his pillow. I finally coaxed him to come with me to the hospital, where it was *safe*. Bruce did not want to go, but he trusted me. As soon as we arrived, he was restrained and given meds. The delusions quieted but never left; they were simply controlled.

The attending psychiatrist met with me and explained that I had a decision to make. She stated that Bruce suffered a breakdown, but with proper medication and regular therapy, there was a very good possibility that he would recover completely. "You can walk away now," she said, "and I will admit him, or you can choose to help him." The thought of free-spirited Bruce being locked up was horrifying to me, so I agreed to the plan, and, less than a month later,

I took Bruce as my husband—for better, for worse, for richer, for poorer, in sickness and in health. Wedding guests thought his rapid speech and odd statements at the reception were from drinking too much, but Bruce was much too fragile to drink and too medicated to know the difference.

Bruce never fully regained his former equilibrium. He remained paranoid and irrational; however, there were days, sometimes weeks, when he enjoyed life. He was especially elated when I became pregnant. "I'm going to be a dad!" he exuberantly told strangers on the street. At the local grocery store, before we knew the gender of the baby, he bought a small, brightly colored ball. That forty-nine-cent toy carried the heartfelt hope that someday we would be a family.

On a hazy summer evening, while we were attending Mass at a church near the university, my labor began. Ten hours later, baby Matt arrived. The moment the nurse handed him to me to hold, I fell in love. He was beautiful—perfect in all ways. Bruce was happy too, but his happiness was more akin to pride than joy; he'd boast that he was a father and brandish Matt like a high school achievement award. Bruce loved Matt, but the medication left him detached and disengaged.

When Bruce's symptoms subsided, his love of writing reawakened. He enrolled in a creative writing program at a university in Indiana. No sooner had he done so, though, than he suffered a severe psychotic episode and slowly faded into a world of bizarre and torturous thoughts. He deeply wanted to be *normal*, but the world in which he lived would not release its grip. As the months passed, Bruce's erratic episodes became increasingly alarming, even with medication. He could not be left alone—it was dangerous. I hid our knives because he threatened to mutilate himself, and I locked up medications so that he would not overdose. Even driving him to the doctor was precarious, because he tried to leap from the car while it was moving. Finally, the psychiatrist determined that Bruce had to be committed, explaining that he was irretrievably insane. For the first time, we had a diagnosis: paranoid schizophrenia with obsessive-compulsive traits. "There is no choice," the doctor said matter-of-factly. "He must be confined for his own good and yours."

I was heartbroken. What began as a love story ended as a tragedy. I was widowed by insanity.

Matt was just a toddler when his father lay straitjacketed in the psychiatric ward of the local hospital. Though we visited Bruce daily, as time passed, our trips became perfunctory; we were there, but Bruce was in another world, a very scary world of strange visions and incoherent ranting. Matt didn't understand what was going on, but whenever he saw the hospital, he would point and say, "Daddy lives there."

Matt was the living gift from this ill-fated marriage, the progeny of a love now vacant. He was both my companion and my comfort. His giggles made me laugh; his cuddles filled my emptiness. With playthings in tow, we'd walk to the park to frolic in the sand and swing high into the air. "Pretty," he would say as he looked at the sunset; it was his first real word.

One late afternoon, we took a different path and strode to a friend's home. We had been invited to a barbecue, and it was there that we met Ron. He had recently returned from Europe, where he had been vacationing with his girlfriend. She had passed away unexpectedly while they traveled through France, and he had returned to the United States prematurely with her remains. Friends supported Ron in those early months, offering him kindness, a place to stay, and food to eat. Though his parents lived in the same town, Ron was not welcome in their home because of his long-standing friction with his father.

Friends introduced Ron to me, but it was our separate vulnerabilities and burdens that drew us together. While Ron mourned the loss of his girlfriend, I mourned the loss of a marriage. I was securing a divorce from Bruce while working at the university; Ron was piecing together his life while finishing his senior year. Each of us thought we could help the other. And neither of us was willing to look beyond the immediacy of our situation. We wanted to escape our pain—not face it. Like two magnets in a storm, we found each other.

One day, Ron met me as I walked home from work.

"Hey," he said as he jumped out from behind a tree, laughing heartily at my obvious surprise. He wrapped his arms around me and pulled me down to the grass, where he kissed me passionately. "This has to be better than work," he exclaimed.

"I couldn't agree more," I replied, still laughing from the surprise.

I really did not know Ron, but I desperately wanted normalcy. Handsome, charismatic, and fun-loving, he was a breath of fresh air. It felt wonderful to laugh again. And as we romped in the grass and watched the clouds float across the sky, I fell in love.

Ron frequently visited the library where I worked and would walk home with me at the close of business. Little Matt was always excited to see Ron. "Hi, big man," Ron would say to him as he picked him up, throwing Matt into the air, eliciting squeals of delight. Sometimes Ron took him to the local carousel, where he rode the wooden ponies. Within weeks of meeting him, Matt began calling Ron Daddy, his biological father slipping silently into oblivion.

During those first months of dating, I lived in a fantasy world of young love. Whenever a doubt surfaced, I ignored it. When anyone questioned me about something Ron said or did, I ended the friendship. In my world, Ron was flawless, and I needed to protect that image—even from my own mounting reservations.

When Ron told me about his friend who was taking his physics exams for him, I accepted his explanation, even though I knew this was a serious offense in the academic world. When he told me about some of the pranks that he pulled on people in the town, I laughed uncomfortably at the stories. When he bragged about stealing liquor and other items from households in the neighborhood, I reasoned it was just a matter of "boys will be boys" and ignored my apprehension. I was blindly attracted to Ron, and the blindness was of my own making. I chose blind love over desolation.

Six months after meeting each other, Ron and I married. Both sets of parents tried unsuccessfully to dissuade us from rushing into a legal commitment, but we were determined to begin a new life. We were inseparable; we were a family. When we located an empty farmhouse about ten miles from the university, we met with the owners and agreed to fix up the house in exchange for rent. Cows grazed in the pastures next to the house while geese waddled through the yard. It was the postcard-perfect embodiment of wholesome country living, a dream come true.

When we moved in, though, something shifted.

Away from the university, away from family and friends, we were alone—two troubled adults and a lively toddler. We busied ourselves with common chores and maintained our responsibilities at the university, but we could not avoid each other. It is difficult to hold on to a fantasy when you confront reality, and as our dream of an idyllic life dissolved, the violence began.

I never understood it; from the beginning, it was consistently inconsistent. Without provocation or obvious cause, Ron could erupt in a fury of accusations and threats. His voice would become louder and dense with emotion as he glared at me through squinted eyes. "What did you do?" he said, pushing me backward, one shove after another. "Who do you think you are? Huh?"

Ron usually apologized after episodes like this and said he loved me, which evoked my sympathy and understanding. He had shared stories of how his father had abused him when Ron was a child, and I reasoned that his reactions were the result of this mistreatment, or perhaps his way of managing frustration.

During the first months of our marriage, I sincerely believed that Ron did not intend to scare or hurt me. His outbursts did not happen every day, even though his disparaging remarks became commonplace. That said, Ron could be quite playful and lighthearted. We had a pony, which he loved to ride in the fields, often taking Matt with him. He even brought the pony into the house—just to enjoy my shocked reaction. He was childlike in that way. Nevertheless, as time passed and the flare-ups continued, I slowly grew more cautious, more tentative, until finally fear became a part of my life.

We had a large vegetable garden, the produce of which we shared with neighbors and friends. During the hot Indiana summer, we had to water the plants regularly. One day I good-naturedly squirted Ron. He grabbed the hose from me, knocked me to the ground, and stuck the hose in my mouth so that I could not breathe. I struggled to get away but could not. A friend was visiting, and he ran to assist. He was horrified by what he saw. "What are you *doing*?" he yelled. Ron did not answer him, but threw the hose to the ground as he walked away. Embarrassed, I muttered, "Ron is having a bad day," and continued watering the vegetables. The friend looked at me in disbelief.

On another occasion, Ron was frustrated with our well pump, which had stopped working for the second time. He came into the house and began cursing and backed me against the wall. Holding me there, he slugged the wall on either side of my face with his fists. I cringed as he hit, which fueled his rage. When he broke through the Sheetrock in several places, he also glazed my cheek. I was terrorized at the thought of being beaten. Finally, he hit a stud and broke his hand.

I drove Ron to the hospital, and when the doctor examined his hand, he pointedly asked, "Who did you hit?" Ron explained that he had fallen. "You expect me to believe that?" the doctor retorted. "Breaks like this are from fights. Who did you hit?" he asked again. The doctor looked over at me, but I said nothing. Ron kept to his story and decided never to return to that doctor.

Ron had not met my family, so for our first Christmas together we decided to make the long drive from Indiana to California to be with them. We loaded up my Volkswagen Beetle, which I had purchased after graduating from college, and started on our way. Matt slept soundly in the backseat. After a number of hours, I was surprised that he was still asleep; he was normally quite active and inquisitive. Finally, I brought up my concerns to Ron, explaining that something must be wrong—maybe Matt was sick. Ron's response sent chills through me.

"I gave him extra cough medicine to make him sleep," Ron said irritably.

"You did what?" I frantically responded as I turned to shake Matt, who sleepily roused.

"I'm not going to drive with a fussy baby!" Ron said. "It's always a big deal with you, isn't it? Always a big deal!"

"He's a baby!" I cried. "You can't just medicate him because you don't want him to speak!"

"I'm tired of your emotionality!" Ron retorted. "My family warned me you were damaged goods, and they were right! They were right!"

When we arrived at my family's farm, Ron was outwardly gracious to them, but behind closed doors, it was a different matter. My parents noticed neither Ron's underlying judgments about their way of life nor my growing discomfort about being there. They were preoccupied with their first grandchild, for whom they had purchased a child-size, authentically replicated tractor. The entire family watched gleefully as Matt learned to maneuver around the yard, pedaling awkwardly at first, then with vigor. They were having as much fun as he was; they all shrieked with laughter at his every twist and turn.

Saying good-bye was both a sorrow and a relief. I love being with my family; I relax with them. But being with them while managing Ron's displeasure tore me up inside. I ached to escape, to run barefoot down the country road next to the farm, to the canal where I sat dreaming as a child. Since that was not possible, I welcomed the journey home. When the time came to finally bid farewell, I was ready.

"Glad that's over," Ron said as we drove away. "Now I know why you act like such a hick. You grew up with hicks!"

"They're farmers," I explained. "Hardworking, good people."

"Look at the facts, Gwen," he continued. "They're Okies! Your mom thinks dinner is warming up hot dogs!"

I felt humiliated and realized that I was not good enough for Ron. It was useless to explain that Mom fixed dinner for a dozen or more people at a time: sometimes she prepared a roast; sometimes she prepared hot dogs and beans. Ultimately, she cooked the food that she had available at the time.

The unraveling of my storybook fantasy of having the perfect family had a dangerous twist. Rather than see the controlling behavior for what it was, I focused on what must be wrong with me. When Ron referred to me as "stupid" or "incompetent," I didn't think about the fact that I was the one providing for our family; instead, I felt ashamed for not being as smart as he. When he mockingly called me "ugly," I didn't think about Bruce's comments that I was beautiful; rather, I shrank inside, embarrassed to be me. Ron's constant berating encaged my heart as effectively as any prison confines a criminal. I accepted his critiques of me as real, and when he faulted me for his abusive actions, I thought he must be right. After all, his explanation had logic to it: he magnanimously was trying to love me in spite of my failures. I caused the violence, he explained, through my own ineptitude. Try as I did, though, I never understood.

After we had lived on the outskirts of the university for nearly a year, Ron met me at work one day in a pickup. He had traded my VW for the camper-top truck so that we could travel cheaply across the country, without even asking me if it would be acceptable. He had decided that we should move to Canada that summer and become naturalized citizens. Though I asked him how he could have done this without consulting me, I did not press the issue. I loved my car, but I feared Ron's reaction more, so I gave notice to the university and began making preparations for the move. Soon after that, we packed our bags and crossed into Manitoba. About a week later, we landed on Salt Spring Island in British Columbia.

Unlike many US citizens in Canada, we did not move there to

avoid the draft. Before I knew Ron, he had gone to a psychologist who was supportive of draft dodgers. This psychologist provided the Selective Service with evidence that Ron was Class 4-F: not suitable for military service under the established mental standards. I did not know what to think of this, but I was sympathetic to Ron's fear of being drafted, even though many in my family had served in the military, as had Ron's father.

We rented a rustic cabin on the island, just a short walk to the water. The cabin had a wood-burning cooking stove, running water in the kitchen, and an outhouse. Ron tried to find work, but other than randomly assisting with someone's home project, there was none. As his frustration grew, he took it out on me. On one occasion, he shoved me against the kitchen wall and pressed a fork to my face. With the prongs pointing ominously into my cheek, he started his rant about my hillbilly family. As he had done many times before, he mocked me for being a nobody, a farmer's daughter. I spoke up and said, "What about your family?" This one question escalated his fury, and he started yelling more loudly, claiming he would slice my face with the fork. Finally, he threw the fork, then picked up the kitchen table and hurled it through the picture window. He hit the remaining glass with his fist.

Matt was taking a nap in the bedroom, which was at the other end of the cabin. He heard the crashes and yelled, "Mommy, Mommy, what's happening? I'm scared!"

I responded, "Everything is fine, sweetheart. Just stay in bed. *Don't* get up!" With his hand now bloodied, Ron was calming down. I bandaged his hand with gauze and tape, and he took off in the truck. Matt called out again, "Mommy, I'm scared." I cuddled him in my arms and reassured him that everything was fine, then collapsed on a nearby chair. When Ron returned a few hours later, he acted as though nothing had ever happened. He picked up Matt, playfully wrestled with him, and then began reading a book to him. The two were absorbed in the story when I explained that I was going to take a walk and left.

The sun was low in the sky when I started up the mountain path. I barely noticed the shadows or my surroundings, consumed as I was by my own anguish. Climbing along the rocks, I lost sight of time and got stuck midway up the mountainside. When I noticed the treacherous water far below and the precipice far above, I finally realized the peril that lay before me. It was a curious moment, one of dark clarity. I could not go forward or backward, or so I thought, and yet I knew no fear. I contemplated odd things, like how long it might take for someone to find my dead body, or that my body might never be found. Either way, it did not matter to me in that moment. It was as though I was suspended in time and place, suspended in a vortex of despair. I hung there, not caring if I lived or died. Emotion itself abandoned me.

I had not prayed for quite some time, and in fact, I did not know what I believed in terms of the divine. There was little hope in my world, and prayer seemed artificial at best. With the toes of my shoes supporting me on a narrow rocky ledge, I stretched and gripped the rocks above me. In that awkward position, I made my peace. "Dear God—if there is a God—please help me." The only sadness I felt was for Matt. I wondered what his life would be like without me. Would it be better, as Ron had claimed? And so I prayed again: "Dear God, if you hear me, please take care of Matt." With that, I decided to move, and if I fell, so be it.

To my astonishment, I made it up the mountain almost without difficulty. I wondered why or how, but there were no answers. It was a mystery to me. I thought about this all the way back to the cabin. How could I have climbed that vertical mountainside so easily when I hadn't been able to move a few minutes before? Was I helped? Did God hear me? I never told Ron where I had gone or what had happened. As with many things, I kept this experience to myself.

We were on Salt Spring Island only a few months before Ron decided he wanted to move to Japan to study Zen Buddhism. We had met a Zen master when we were at the university, and he had invited us to study with him in Niigata, Japan. Ron determined that now was the time. To make this trip, however, we needed funds. Incredibly, Ron wanted me to contact my parents to ask if we could work and stay with them. When I called, they were happy to help and invited us to come down. We stayed at the farm for the next several months. Ron worked for my father; I found a job as a secretary.

I pretended that all was well, but I couldn't breathe. It was as if I were in a mechanical vice, pressed by expectations—those of Ron and those of my parents. Ron had given me the ultimatum, and my heart pounded at my distress, my lungs clutched at my terror. I could not speak.

"I swear, I'm taking Matt!" he sneered. "You'll come home some day and he won't be here! I'm going to take him and leave. Then what are you going to do, huh?"

I was profoundly frightened that Ron would make good on his threat, and began hyperventilating. My family rushed me to the hospital, thinking I was having a heart attack. The heart palpitations intensified as I obsessed about when and how Ron might abduct Matt. I could not share the reasons for my distress, because such disclosure could have a terrible end.

So severe was my anxiety that I had to quit my job. The phone would ring, and I'd panic before I even answered it, frightened that I would hear that Matt was gone. My parents did not know what to think about my behavior, but they realized that something was not right. They had never seen me like this before.

At my family's urging, I went to a doctor. He prescribed medications for anxiety, told me to rest, and advised me not to travel because of my level of distress. I neither took the medication nor rested, because I was too afraid of what might happen if I fell asleep.

After several months at the farm, we sold the pickup and paid for our airline tickets. Through a friend of the Zen master, we were also able to obtain work visas. My parents drove us to the airport, and, with duffel bags in tow, we were on our way. Just before we got on the plane, my mother put $300 in my pocket. Her gift was a lifesaver, because we were traveling with only a few dollars in our possession.

When we arrived in Japan, Ron contacted the Zen master whom we had met at the university. Sensei, as he was called, introduced us to a few people, and they helped us find a place to live. Initially we shared housing with several other foreigners; later, we moved into a small house in the outcast district of Niigata. Though this area was considered a ghetto, the dwellings were modest and clean. The home we rented was comfortable and adequate for our needs.

Sensei met with us weekly for group meditation and also for training in the ancient Japanese art of tea ceremony, a beautiful, meditative ritual designed to bring participants into silence. According to Sensei, the practice of tea ceremony was one of the most effective means to spiritual awakening. He offered the classes in his small office on the third floor of the university's administration building. The office adjoined another small room, where Sensei had a table and a few chairs; Matt played in this room with his superhero toys while we practiced tea. The door was always open between the two rooms, and Matt wandered back and forth at will. Sometimes he even joined us for part of the ceremony.

One day while practicing tea, I suddenly felt imminent danger for Matt. I jumped up and ran into the next room. Matt had pushed a chair over to the window and was standing on the ledge. I talked softly and cheerfully to distract him, as I moved quickly to his side. Matt excitedly explained that he was going to fly like his favorite ninja toy. I responded, "But Mommy's got a *big* surprise for you: a *new* ninja!" This got his attention, and he turned and reached for me, leaping into my arms. Trembling, I held him tight as I closed the window.

I didn't know how to understand the premonition that ultimately saved Matt's life. Why had I known that Matt was in danger? What could explain the sensation that I had felt? I thought back to my mother's description of guardian angels, and I wondered if one had intervened.

Ron's pleasure at being in Japan was short-lived, and he became increasingly impatient and unhappy. He believed that everyone was staring at him, and this was probably an accurate perception, because in the 1970s there were very few foreigners in the area. We were a novelty—fascinating children and adults alike.

Both of us taught English to support ourselves. At the time, a native English speaker with a degree qualified a person to teach English. We taught at universities and businesses, and also taught privately in our house. Together, we made enough to support ourselves.

Ron's primary interest was the practice of Zen. He focused arduously on enlightenment and spent much time in meditation. He wanted silence and no distractions. Our little home was a traditional one, with sliding paper doors, tatami mats, and interconnecting rooms. Even the slightest sound was audible from any point within the structure. Outside sounds reached inside just as easily as inside sounds stretched outdoors. Complete silence was not possible, and this fact pushed Ron over the edge on several occasions.

"Can't you see I'm meditating?" he yelled. "Keep Matt quiet!"

I quickly went to Matt, who was playing in an adjoining room with his ninja figures.

"Let's go to the park, Matt. I know a perfect spot." I whispered.

"Will you play with me?" Matt asked innocently, and of course I told him I would. Matt was excited and grabbed my hand, but not before Ron shouted again.

"I said *quiet*! You're such poor excuse for a mother," he said with frustration.

"I'm taking Matt outside to play," I responded.

"Of course you are," he sneered. "You'll make him a queer for sure!"

Ron genuinely understood himself to be the victim, even though he was the one inflicting the pain. We were a burden, an albatross around his neck. He had a goal, and that goal did not include us. When he lashed out at either of us, he reeled against the circumstances of his life, against his failed dreams, his lost youth, and his turbulent past.

On one occasion when Matt was playing, Ron exploded and chased him up to the attic room, hitting him as he ran. I ran up after Ron, shouting for him to stop. There was no logical reason for his abusive actions, but he justified them nonetheless. Matt's screams reverberated throughout our home and broke my heart, but Ron simply went back to his meditation.

During our first years in Japan, I also practiced meditation and studied the Zen art of flower arrangement. Through the latter, I became very aware of space—the space between stems and leaves, the space between the flowers and stalks. This minimalist medium drew me into beauty and silence. When I met with Sensei, I explained my experiences with both meditative approaches. And finally, I shared that Ron and I were having difficulty in the marriage. I did not mention the violence. Sensei listened carefully and then drew a large circle and put Ron in the center of this circle. He explained that I needed to surround Ron with detached love, and that I was not to try to change him, confront him, or even worry about how he might or might not respond. Rather, I was to foster interior silence by letting go of the noise of my fear and shame. As I followed his counsel, I began to know peace of mind. I stopped obsessing about Ron and started focusing on my interests. As I grew calmer, it seemed that Ron did as well.

Shortly after that meeting, I had an unexpected religious experience. The back of our home opened up to a tiny garden with a small fishpond. As I sat on the floor, staring at the garden, I was spontaneously caught up in the brilliance of everything around me. My eyes darted from one rock to another, from bees to flowers, from clouds to trees, and I saw that all creation pulsed with the same Life. Inanimate and animate, it was the same. I understood in that instance that ultimately creation is energy. I thought of Sensei and the reverence he offered to the objects in his room. I understood why he bowed to his tea bowl, why he greeted everyone as though they were royalty. I was in awe of what I was seeing, of what I was beginning to understand. I did not know what to call my experience, but I knew it to be beyond anything I had ever known before. The only word that seemed to capture what I was realizing was *God*, and so it was that I called this transcendent awareness—God. By naming it, I opened an important door.

Filled with the desire to know more about the God I was experiencing, I went into the house to find the small New Testament that a Protestant missionary had left us. It was in the closet, stacked alongside various boxes and toys. I picked it up, returned to the garden, and began to read. I got only as far as Matthew 11:28–30 before my heart opened further. The passage read:

Come to me, all you who are weary and find life burdensome, and I will refresh you. Take my yoke upon your shoulders and learn from me, for I am gentle and humble of heart. Your soul will find rest, for my yoke is easy and my burden light.

After reading these verses, I *saw* Jesus in front of me, pointing to his heart, which emanated light. This glimpse was accompanied by rushes of images of me from early childhood onward. Because of what I was seeing, I understood that I was loved, that I was not a mistake, and that I had never been alone. I was overcome with a poignant joy, a joy that honored all that preceded it.

After this mystical encounter, I sought out missionaries in the area: Baptist, Catholic, Lutheran, Methodist, and Presbyterian. Thousands of miles away from their homes and their congregations, the missionaries had put aside their theological differences and bonded with one another. They met regularly for prayer and fellowship, and I became part of their interdenominational community. I never felt pressured to join one church or another; rather, I felt supported to follow my own spiritual path. Their loving acceptance of me extended to my family and was deeply healing.

Over dinner one evening, the Presbyterian minister and his wife shared their story.

"We lost our only son when we served in Bolivia," he said. "His fever spiked, and we tried everything we could to bring it down. I even gave him mouth-to-mouth resuscitation, but it was too late."

"It was his time," his wife said softly. "God called our beautiful child home." Then, turning to me, she added, "Because of this, we tell our friends to have several children. You never know if they will live a full life."

"We were assigned to Japan after his death," the minister continued. "It was a big move for us, but we've come to love the country and the people. We return home every three years for a visit, so I guess *this* is our home."

Stories such as the above were repeated, in one form or another, in the missionary community. Each couple or family had its sorrows and joys, but always it was their faith that guided them. As we became more involved with this ecumenical group, the tensions in our household softened. We now had an extended family to whom we could turn for guidance, for fellowship.

One of the members of this group was Father George. "So, you are Catholics?" he asked one day.

"Well, we were raised Catholic, but we haven't been practicing for quite a few years," I said timidly.

"No worries," he laughed. "Once a Catholic, always a Catholic." And with that declaration, Father George adopted us, inviting us to his rectory, to parties for Catholics in the area, and to other events he thought we might enjoy. We were his family now.

It was as though we were given a new lease on life: through our missionary friends, we had direction and support. During this important juncture, I became pregnant with our second child and only daughter. Though it was a little worrisome to plan for a birth in a foreign setting, our friends were nearby to assist, helping us find a maternity clinic and the baby items we needed. The local people also came to our aid, making sure that I was resting and prepared for the arrival. Matt was seven years old when he became a proud big brother. Little Sarah, with her Gerber Baby smile, swept him and everyone else off their feet.

We spent several years in Japan, before traveling to upstate New York at the invitation of a Catholic missionary organization. It was there that Ron earned a degree in theology and subsequently taught at the seminary. I also earned a degree in theology and worked with the lay associates. This missionary community, like our friends and family, was unaware of the problems in our household.

Ron was charming, self-confident, and articulate. He was a natural teacher, and quickly garnered the admiration of the ordained faculty. I was Ron's soft-spoken wife, who usually had a toddler in her arms. People wanted to believe in us, just as much as we wanted to believe that the image we projected of being a happy, loving family was real. Ron had his role; I had mine. We played our parts quite successfully, for not even we understood the truth of our relationship. Though we both had studied the principles of social justice, we did not link the inherent right of human dignity to our marriage. Ron attacked when frustrated, and I withdrew. Ultimately, it was an unholy and unwholesome alliance.

When Sarah was five years old, Andrew was born. Robust from the moment he arrived, he was the embodiment of his name—strong. Three years later, Johnny followed. Both boys brought immeasurable delight but also busyness. Four children and two working parents is a challenge, and in our household, any additional strain carried the possibility of threat.

The physical abuse during this time was less frequent than in our younger years, but when the violence did occur, it was devastating.

One day I was in the bedroom with baby Johnny. Ron came in yelling, accusing me of undermining him. I put Johnny in the crib and came back into the bedroom. Ron pushed me repeatedly and shoved me onto the bed. In his rage, he picked up the side of the mattress and, with me on it, tossed it across the room. I hit the wall; the mattress followed. Thankfully, I had put the baby in the crib.

When Johnny was seven months old, I went to get groceries while Ron cared for him. As soon as I returned, Ron left quickly for happy hour at the seminary. Johnny was whimpering and lying on the carpet. When I picked him up to nurse him, I noticed something terribly wrong with his head: one side was mushy, like bread dough. I had never seen anything like it. I called the seminary and told them it was an emergency. "Please find Ron and tell him it is urgent that he come home immediately." Ron was aggravated when he arrived.

"What do you want now?" he demanded.

"Look at Johnny's head! What happened? Why is his head this way?" I cried.

"He fell, that's all!" Ron retorted. "Stop making a big deal out of nothing." He turned to leave.

"Why didn't you say something? Why didn't you take him to the doctor?" I interjected.

Ron was very irritated, but I insisted that he go with me to the doctor. When the doctor examined Johnny, she explained that his skull was fractured and the underlying fluid had seeped through. She added that he would need to be checked when he was older, because adhesions could form on the brain. She looked at us directly and asked, "What happened?" Ron explained that Johnny had fallen down the stairs. She didn't ask any more questions, but she told us to watch him carefully, keep him calm, and take him to the hospital if we noticed anything different or had any concerns.

Johnny's head did not return to normal for some time. Perhaps he *had* fallen down the stairs, but I had my doubts. There were no other signs of injuries on his little body, and I was haunted by images of his being hit or thrown. Regardless of how the damage had occurred, though, I had other concerns. Ron had left his injured son on the floor to join his colleagues for happy hour. How could he have done this? Why were his associates more important than his own child?

Over time, violence mixed with the language of love extracts a terrible toll. In my case, I did not know what to believe. Ron loved me; he loved the kids. He told us so. He meant it—didn't he? He would not intentionally hurt us—would he? I had no answers for my questions, and the questions themselves were so frightening for me that I buried them deep inside. Only later did I realize that I feared love as much as I feared violence. They were the same.

I lived on edge, vigilant for the children and for me. Nothing was as it seemed. I smiled to the outside world even when I was crying inside, even when I was frightened, even when I was in despair. I smiled when I felt I had to smile, when I felt I was expected to. I tried to please everyone and never considered myself. Unfortunately, not only do such facades cover the torments below the surface; they also envelop our hearts until only numbness remains. Once this occurs, something dies inside—something very vital.

A friend invited me to accompany her to a workshop on healing. As part of the process, we were asked to bring a baby photo of ourselves. As we sat in a semicircle, the leaders explained the biblical roots of healing and invited us to pray. Once the group prayer ended, they walked around the room and prayed over each member individually. After completing the circle, the leaders spoke of their prayer experience with the group and what they felt in terms of the movement of the Spirit in each person's life. They spoke rather generally at first but then became quite specific, saying that one person in the group had a broken heart. They stated that it was as if the heart were "shattered in little pieces" and "held together with tape and string." Since I didn't know most of the members, I had no idea whom they were addressing, but I was soon to find out.

At the close of the workshop, the leaders offered to pray with each of us alone in a separate room. When it was my turn, I went to the back room with little more than simple curiosity. Both leaders were standing when I walked in. They greeted me gently and lovingly and then explained that I was the one with the shattered heart.

"It is as though you have suffered so much that your heart now barely functions," they explained. "Do you understand?"

"No," I said simply. "I don't know what you mean."

"Look at the baby photo you brought today, Gwen," they said tenderly. "See how happy she is? What happened between then and now?"

I stared at the cute-little-girl me, but I still could not grasp what they were intimating. I felt nothing—nothing at all.

"I don't know what to say," I responded. "There have been difficulties, but everyone has problems."

"Not everyone has a shattered heart because of their problems, Gwen. What happened?"

"I am sorry, I don't know what you mean," I replied again, feeling increasingly perplexed. I knew I was disappointing them; I knew they wanted me to realize something, but I genuinely did not know what it was that they hoped I would see.

The healers prayed with me, that I might understand and might receive the healing they felt I needed. As tender as they were with me, I still left the room without any sense of connection with what I had been told. There was no resonance in my heart, no emotional response of any kind, certainly no understanding.

My days were jam-packed with the details of living—the demands of work, the needs of the family. There was no time to be self-reflective about the little girl in the photo. I was busy trying to live the dream that I had envisioned since adolescence—my husband and children happy, our home beautifully decorated, our meals wholesomely prepared—and that guided me, prompting me to work into the night when I needed to. I wanted this dream so much that I could not see what was before me—until one fateful December day when everything changed.

We had a lovely Christmas tree front and center in our picture window. The children and I strung popcorn and cranberries and placed the garlands on the tree, which we'd decorated with glass bulbs and a variety of handmade ornaments. They delighted in imagining what this Christmas might bring. Andrew and Johnny both wanted bicycles and Transformer toys; Sarah wanted anything related to music and ballet. She dreamed of new pointe shoes and leotards. She'd swirl about the house, rehearsing scenes from *The Nutcracker*, while imagining herself to be a prima ballerina.

Unlike on prior Christmases, when gifts had been hidden about the house until Christmas Eve, this year I made the unfortunate decision to put some of the wrapped gifts under the tree a week earlier. The brightly colored packages added to the festivity and the excitement in the household. I mistakenly thought the children were old enough to resist the temptation to peek, but it was hard to contain the boys' curiosity, and they pleaded that they be able to open just one. Sadly, Andrew tried to do just that.

I was enrolled in a certification program for counselors, and the last class was just before Christmas. Ron stayed with the children while I went to this class. The meetings were held in the home of the two psychologists providing the training. The session began with a documentary film about Joseph Campbell, the noted mythologist. Discussion followed, but I listened only halfheartedly because I was mesmerized by all the images of angels around the room—paintings and unique stone and ceramic figurines from their travels. While looking at these images, I suddenly felt an overwhelming sense of dread, and I knew Andrew was in jeopardy. Because the premonition was so compelling, I turned to my colleague and whispered, "I've got to go. My son is in danger. Please explain to the group." I left immediately.

I drove home in a panic. I *knew* Ron had somehow hurt Andrew.

When I ran into the house, I saw Ron on the phone. He was laughing and talking to someone. Over his laughter, I heard Sarah's screams. When she saw me, she ran to me and pulled me into her bedroom. Johnny was in the corner, huddled and sobbing behind the bed. Andrew rested with his back against a dresser, bent over at a ninety-degree angle. He was gasping for air.

Sarah cried, "Dad kicked him many times in the stomach, Mom. He knocked him across the room. He picked Andrew up, held him by his shoulders, and kneed him so hard that Andrew flew across the room!"

Sarah continued to cry hysterically while I knelt beside Andrew. He could not speak; he could not straighten up. I checked him for obvious external injuries and faced my own terror—should I call 911? I held Andrew and listened carefully to his breathing. Slowly, very slowly, his diaphragm relaxed, and just as slowly, he began to breathe more easily. While I held Andrew, Sarah explained what had happened.

Andrew had been looking at the wrapped presents under the tree, when he spotted one marked for him. Thinking no one would notice, he sneaked behind the tree to unravel the end of a package—just to get a quick peek at what might be inside. He unknowingly chose a package of rocks, which went with a rock tumbler that was still wrapped. Ron found out about this transgression and became enraged. He grabbed Andrew and gave free rein to his anger, beating and kicking him, berating him for what he had done, all the while feeling justified in his actions. After all, our eight-year-old son had opened one end of a wrapped Christmas gift a few days early.

My heart pounded and my mind raced as I tried to comfort Andrew. I didn't know if his injuries were serious or not, but I wanted to take him to the doctor. I wanted to call the police. I wanted someone to help. I knew, however, that any action on my part would mean front-page news because of Ron's prominence in the community. And I knew Ron would react even more violently. A phone call would mean the end of our family as we knew it.

When Ron got off the phone, Sarah started yelling at him. "I hate you! I hate you!" she screamed. His response was simple: he ordered her to "get a grip" and told the rest of us to stop exaggerating. Turning to me, he yelled, "This is just like you, making something out of nothing. It was Andrew's fault—he got what he deserved!" Then he walked out of the house.

He never checked Andrew, never asked how he was feeling, never listened to his breathing. He did not care. He simply walked out of the house and slammed the door. I realized at that moment, at the sound of that slamming door, that I hated him. My excuses for his violence, because of what he supposedly endured as a child, ended on that ill-fated day.

Andrew's breathing slowly returned to normal, but he was greatly shaken by the assault and did not speak. Johnny ran to me once Ron left the house. He was still crying as he clung to my leg. Sarah was sobbing as well and repeatedly shouted that she hated her father. As I comforted my children, my mind raced through the valleys of my despondency and the leveled mountains of my dreams. How was I going to resolve this calamity?

In this moment, the lessons I had been taught growing up about facing adversity and finding solutions, about enduring pain and suffering with dignity, were too clouded by my fear and anger to ring true. How could Ron have done this to Andrew? It was one thing for him to lash out at me, quite another for him to hurt our child.

All of us make mistakes. All of us have regrets. There is nothing I regret more than not having called 911 on that cold December day. That said, I am not sure that such a call would have been the better choice. My heart might have been temporarily freer, but the consequence of that action might have left the children even more traumatized. As many times as I have rehearsed this drama, I still have no answer—except that I did the best I could at the time.

Later that evening, Ron returned home. Unbeknownst to me, Andrew had written an apology and placed it in our bedroom. Ron took this as evidence that he had acted appropriately. When I read the message, it brought me to tears. A child was lovingly apologizing for being a child.

The physical attack on Andrew was a turning point in our home. Christmas Day was rather somber. We didn't laugh much as we opened our presents. We acted as though the beating had never happened, but we all knew differently. Not surprisingly, Andrew never played with his rock tumbler. It was stored in the garage until many years later, when we gave it to another child. Because of what had happened, I could no longer pretend that everything was okay. I was finally awakened from my deadened state. I told the children one by one that no matter who was being hit and no matter what the reason, if their father ever got violent again, they were to call the police, and certainly I would do the same. This arrangement became a reality when we went to a wedding in upstate New York. Ron started a physical fight with Matt, who began bleeding from his lips. I screamed for them to stop and picked up the phone and started dialing the police. When Ron saw me do so, he ended the fight.

Shortly afterward, I took Andrew to see a social worker. Andrew shared a repetitive nightmare he was having. In this dream, he was falling—through his bed, through the floors in the house, deep into a dark abyss. He talked about the beating, the terror he felt, and the sense of rejection. By the time the session concluded, he was laughing, something he had not done freely since the attack.

The children were unaware of Ron's physical abuse of me, or so I thought. I didn't let anyone know about my circumstances, wearing clothes that covered the bruises and remaining quiet when the attacks occurred. Only my physicians and counselors knew about the domestic violence, and without exception, these professionals urged me to divorce Ron. I realized after Andrew's beating that I might have to take that step, but it was a frightening prospect. As a

Catholic, I judged myself harshly for the failure of my marriage—doubly so because I had been married briefly before. I felt terribly alone in my suffering—until the visitation.

Ron's rage toward me always erupted unexpectedly, except this time. He found out that I had instructed the children to call 911 if there was violence. I knew he would retaliate, and he did. He walked into the bedroom and closed the door, an action that always sent chills through my body. He began shoving me, saying that I didn't support him in front of the kids. Grabbing my hair and yanking me toward him, he sneered, "Who do you think you are, huh, nigger?" I tried to push him away, but he grasped my breasts so firmly that he scratched them through my clothing. Finally, he threw me on the bed, straddled my body, and began choking me. I could not breathe; I could not move. I thought I would surely die. As I slipped into darkness, he got up and left the room. Curled up on the bed, trying to catch my breath, I felt very, very alone. I could not imagine living much longer. The misery was simply too great. In this place of utter desolation, however, something miraculous occurred.

Suddenly, and without any thought or prayer, I sensed a warm presence beside me. I was lying on my side, and this presence leaned close against my back. It felt human, but no one was in the room with me. To my amazement, I then felt the wings of an angel wrap around me from behind. The wings rested on my arms and fluttered slightly. It was as though I were held by a soft love, and this love spread throughout my entire body. As unfathomable tenderness embraced me, my heart opened, and I let go and sobbed. Like a child in a mother's arms, I was being comforted.

I don't know how long the angel stayed with me, for I had no sense of time. The angel did not speak during this visitation, but it communicated: we are never alone, even in the most devastating circumstances, and, most importantly, we are deeply loved.

At the Foot of the Cross

Our hearts are crowded with secrets, from childhood shenanigans to adolescent indiscretions, from things we've seen to others we've imagined. We tuck away stories and experiences, hiding them from ourselves and others. *What will they think of me if I speak?* we wonder. Disclosure feels too costly, and so, we hold our secrets near. Some haunt us; others soothe us.

The angel's visitation became one of my secrets. I told no one about it, because I did not know how to explain what had occurred without also sharing the context. And my time with the angel was too precious—I could not risk the possibility of its being diminished. When the phone rang one hot summer evening, it was the angel's message—that we are never alone and we are deeply loved—that I held on to.

I was washing the dinner dishes when the call came. My sisters were flying into La Guardia Airport, and I knew it must be from them. This was their first trip to the East Coast, and the three of us had great plans for exploring New York City. Ron offered to pick them up while I stayed home with our youngest two sons, who were already in bed. Matt was traveling through Canada, and Sarah was away at ballet camp. The house was particularly quiet when I answered the phone.

"Hello?" I said, drying my sudsy hands.

"Would you accept a collect call from Sarah?" the operator asked.

"Yes, yes, of course," I replied. "Sarah? Are you there?"

"Mommy... Mommy... Something terrible has happened!" Sarah responded.

I could barely understand her words; her voice was hoarse and muffled by tears. I heard words, phrases, but not sentences.

"Suzie's mother yelled..." Her voice trailed off. "I...scared... fainted..." Sarah was crying.

"I can't hear you well, sweetie. Tell me again, very slowly," I said.

Sarah began again, and I finally understood that she was scared for her roommate, Suzie, who was anorexic. The child was so emaciated that she had fainted several times during the summer and was now lying on her bed, listless. The seriousness of the situation prompted camp counselors to call Suzie's parents and insist that the child be taken home, or camp officials would take her to the hospital.

"When Suzie's mother arrived, she screamed at me, Mommy. She didn't even look at Suzie; she just yelled at me that it was my fault, that I was bad, that I lied when I reported Susie's problem," Sarah sobbed loudly. "It's not true, Mommy! It's not true! I feel so terrible...I feel so terrible."

I tried consoling Sarah, pointing out that the mother, not she, was at fault, but then she blurted out the real problem.

"Mommy, I remembered something horrible when she was screaming at me." She continued, "I remembered my secret of being sexually abused as a little girl."

I could barely hear Sarah, and I thought I must have misunderstood.

"What was that, sweetie? I couldn't hear you," I replied.

"I was sexually abused when I was little, Mommy." Sarah cried haltingly. "I feel so awful, so dirty. I just want to die." Her voice trailed off as she wept.

A paralyzing shock wave of alarm darted through me. Faces, places, emotions fought for my attention as I tried to understand what Sarah had just said, and what I should say in return.

"Sarah, honey, you are beautiful. You are perfect. You have done nothing wrong. Tomorrow morning I'm driving up to get you, so don't worry," I said quickly.

Sarah had slipped away from her ballet group and gone up to the top floor of the dormitory, where she had found an isolated phone booth in which to hide and call me. No one knew she was there.

"I'm scared, Mommy. I'm so scared. What will people say? What will Daddy say?" she cried.

"Everyone will think you are very courageous, Sarah. Everyone. Your dad loves you no matter what," I answered.

"I feel so alone, so ugly." Sarah sobbed, her voice rising and falling.

"I know you do, sweetie, but I am with you. You are not alone. I need to call your counselor now so she can be with you. Can you promise me that you will stay by the phone while I call her?" I asked.

"Okay," she muttered weakly as she cried.

The next twenty minutes stretched into mental hours. I could not locate a counselor, even after calling every floor and wing of the residence hall. Unbeknownst to me, the counselors were with Suzie's mother, who continued to rage at staff and child alike. I finally called the health center staff and reached a nurse willing to locate a counselor to help Sarah. When I called Sarah back, she was still huddled on the floor of the phone booth, not wanting to see anyone. Memories of abuse flooded her consciousness, holding her captive.

"She was a big woman, Mommy, with mean eyes. She had short white hair, and her name was Alice. Sister Alice. Her voice was ugly too. She would change it to a sweet, soft voice when she got me on the table, but it could be real firm," she said.

I thought I remembered this person. And when Sarah described the location of the office, I knew without a doubt who she was.

"You go through the front entrance, Mommy, and walk down the main corridor. That's where her office was—toward the end of the corridor, close to Daddy's office," she explained.

Sarah was still crying, but she would intersperse questions like "Do you think Daddy will be able to look at me, Mommy? Do you think Sister Alice will come after me if I talk? Do you think people can tell by looking at me that I was abused?"

All my years of training as a therapist had not prepared me for this moment. My own child had been victimized, and the reality of that fact left me in shock. Sarah's words slowly broke through my devastation and unleashed an incredible fury. I was determined that justice would be achieved. Very carefully, I asked what Sister Alice had done to her, and how old she had been when it started.

"I was little, about five years old," Sarah said. "She put me on the table and took off my panties and did awful things."

Sarah was crying uncontrollably again, and I asked nothing more. I simply held her on the phone, cried with her, and promised that I would take action. The counselor arrived soon after that and drew Sarah out of the booth and back to her bedroom.

Shortly after I put the receiver down, my sisters arrived. I wanted to share their excitement, I wanted to laugh with them, but my heart pounded so loudly that I could only watch their lips move. Sobs clutched my throat, strangling every breath I took. I was in agony. How could this have happened to my daughter? Why had this woman hurt my child?

While my sisters settled into their room, I told Ron about Sarah's call. He listened carefully, clinched his jaw as he stared into the distance, and said he knew it was Alice. "She's that kind of person," he said. And he agreed that I needed to go pick Sarah up from camp. Then I talked to my sisters, sharing what Sarah had just explained. My sisters and I talked long into the night, comforting each other and bemoaning the tragedies of life, and prepared for the early-morning drive to Saratoga.

At the time when Sarah was being abused, our family lived near a religious community in upstate New York, and Sister Alice had passed by our home every day as she walked to and from work. Many times I greeted her with a simple hello, but she rarely even glanced my way. I wrongly attributed her remoteness to what I perceived to be her frozen lifestyle. When I mentioned her strangeness to Ron, who knew her because they both taught at the seminary, he explained that she was probably preoccupied with her work. Neither of us suspected that Sister Alice's demeanor cloaked madness.

Before sunlight could guide us, my sisters and I drove to the ballet camp in Saratoga. It was the longest four hours I had ever known, but I remember little of it. I was so possessed by Sarah's circumstance that I did not notice the surroundings—or the highway patrolman who stopped me for speeding. When we arrived at the campus, we went directly to the dormitory; counselors were sitting with Sarah, waiting for us. She was pale and withdrawn, her eyes sunken and red-rimmed. She leaped into my outstretched arms. She seemed so frail, so tiny, as I held her close. My heart ached for her—how could anyone hurt such a precious being?

"Mommy," she cried, "Mommy, I feel so awful. I'm scared they will come after me. Do you think they will come after me?"

"No one is going to hurt you, I promise. I'll make sure of it," I said. "It's going to be okay." All the while, I was thinking, *She is saying* they. *There must be more than one abuser!*

My sisters and I took Sarah to the park, hopped on and off the swings, distracted her with ice cream and funny childhood stories, and walked. We offered familiar comfort, family comfort. Sarah's unrelenting concern was about being seen as an ugly person because of what happened. We affirmed her beauty, her courage, and her innocence. That night the four of us snuggled in a local motel, watching old movies until we fell asleep. With her mom and her aunties, Sarah was a child again and felt safe.

The following morning, Sarah attended her scheduled ballet class. From a distance, my sisters and I watched as she performed her exercises at the barre and then elegantly moved into pirouettes. When the class concluded, Sarah ran to us and explained that she wanted to finish the remaining two weeks of camp. She wanted to be with her friends. The counselors supported her request and said they would stay close by to make sure she was okay. Though not convinced, I finally conceded. We tearfully said our good-byes and began the lengthy drive home. Shortly after we arrived, however, Sarah phoned, crying hysterically. She was remembering more.

"Mommy, there were more of them," she sobbed. "There were two priests in the room too. They hurt me so bad, hurt me so bad…" Her voice trailed off incoherently.

While I comforted her, I was in such distress myself that I could not process what I was hearing. I was afraid to ask questions; it was all too shocking. I asked if her counselor was with her—thankfully, she was—and I promised to pick her up in the morning.

The next day, Ron and I drove back to Saratoga to bring our daughter home. While our boys wrestled in the backseat of our old Dodge Dart, we strategized about what to do. We knew Sarah would have to identify her assailants, we knew she would need an attorney, and we knew she would require professional help to heal. We thought of friends we could call for referrals. The boys did not know what had occurred, other than that Sarah was upset, but they were the first to jump out of the car when we finally pulled onto the campus. Seeing their sister, they ran to give her a hug. They all giggled a bit, and then Sarah turned to her dad. She had been very worried that he would not accept her, so when he embraced her and assured her that everything would be okay, she sobbed freely.

Ron and I did not talk much about the abuse after we returned home. He was busy with his work and impatient around tears. The following week, though, we took Sarah to the seminary where Ron had worked when the abuse occurred, so that she could do an in-person identification. At this point, we knew only that Sister Alice was implicated, not who the offending priests were.

We walked into a very large cafeteria where administrators, faculty, and students were eating. Sister Alice was at one of the tables. "There she is," Sarah whispered, pointing to Alice. "She's the one who hurt me." Clearly in distress, Sarah darted outdoors. I quickly followed her, while Ron went to speak with the head of the institution. Sarah spotted her friend across the courtyard and ran over to her, sobbing. I watched as Sarah gestured toward the building, and saw them disappear through the garden entrance. Within minutes, Sarah returned.

"You must come with me, Mommy!" Sarah said with a frozen gaze.

"Where are we going, Sarah?" I asked.

"You must come with me, Mommy!" she demanded, grabbing my hand and pulling me to follow. Seeing her obvious distress, I went with Sarah. I didn't know what to expect.

"Where are we going, Sarah?" I asked again.

"We are going to rip her face off!" Sarah declared.

"What?" I responded.

"We are going to rip her face off! I saw her. I saw her!" she shouted.

Sarah's eyes were frozen straight ahead. She was walking so fast that I was having difficulty keeping pace. I asked her to slow down, but Sarah was deafened by her own rage. She was determined to confront Sister Alice. Pointing directly ahead of us, trembling, Sarah said, "I saw her go in there, Mommy. I'm going into that room and I'm going to rip her face off!"

We were now standing in the corridor of the seminary. There were people walking past us, and they were aware that there was a problem. Sarah was sobbing, her visage ghostly white. I tried to convince her to go back outside with me, but she would not budge. Finally, I suggested we join her father at the meeting. "Daddy is talking with the priest in charge," I explained. "Come with me and tell Daddy and Father who you saw." She agreed.

Sarah looked like a Blythe doll, with huge, sorrowful eyes, when she marched like a soldier to the priest's office. "My husband is meeting with Father," I explained to the receptionist, "and it is important that we see him as well." The receptionist hesitated just long enough for Sarah to snap, "I want to see my daddy!" And with that, we were granted entry.

As we crossed the threshold of the paneled mahogany door leading to the office, terror stole Sarah's resolve. She was once again a five-year-old child. Through heart-wrenching sobs, she relayed how Sister Alice had hurt her and added that she had just seen her down the hall. Wiping away his own tears, the priest struggled to stay composed as he listened to her story. He expressed his regret to Sarah, and then turned to us and stated that he would set up a meeting with Alice.

Five of us—one priest, Sister Alice and her advocate, and Ron and I—met a couple of weeks later in a dimly lit conference room, not far from the site of the atrocities. The priest explained why we were gathered, and then Sister Alice began talking in an eerily sentimental manner. I recalled what Sarah had told me: "Her voice was ugly, but she would change it to a sweet, soft voice." I knew I was hearing what Sarah had heard, when she was just a little child pinned down on Alice's desk. And as I listened, I was transported back in time to the scene of the crime, where I was helpless to do anything. I wanted to scream. I wanted Sister Alice to suffer, but I had to remain focused for the questioning.

The time we spent in this meeting was an introduction to the world of depravity. Sister Alice and her advocate were interested in protecting the organization and the violator, not the truth or the well-being of a child whose life was in shreds.

"I've been thinking about this," Sister Alice said matter-of-factly, pausing at each phrase, "and to do something like this would be... evil, and I'm not evil. I'm not perfect, of course...but I'd never do anything evil."

Her advocate interjected that Alice was a dedicated nun who had served her community for years, and she could not imagine that Alice would do anything like this. Nodding gratefully to her champion, Alice was emboldened and continued with her defense.

"I've never seen a psychologist," Alice stated, "and no one has ever suggested that I see one, so...I must be psychologically healthy. I don't even like children. I feel uncomfortable around them."

Her logic was dumbfounding, but then she turned to her advocate and revealed the extent of her insanity.

"What would this say about my vow of celibacy? Would this violate my vow? What can happen to me if it does?" she asked. "And besides, I'm getting ready to retire. Why should this come up now? It happened a long time ago."

We were stunned. Was this her confession? Even her advocate was taken aback, but she collected herself and responded resolutely, "I'm sure your vow has not been violated!"

"Children have great fantasy lives," Alice asserted. "I've studied psychology, and I know they imagine things. Besides, I don't even know the family; I see Ron sometimes, but that's all."

Alice used a sickeningly saccharine tone throughout the grilling, but there was one notable exception. As the meeting drew to a close, she turned to me, eyes crazed and voice raised.

"I want you to tell Sarah that I am convicted that I did not do it. I am *convicted* that I did not do it! I want you to tell her that! *Be sure to tell her that!*" she exclaimed angrily.

"I assure you, Alice, I *won't* be telling my daughter. Your days of torturing her are over!" I responded passionately.

And then the confession emerged.

We were preparing to leave when Ron commented that sometimes people hurt others unintentionally.

"Oh," Alice responded, squinting her eyes. "I thought you said I *intended* to hurt her. That's different. I never *intended* to hurt Sarah!"

As we stared at her in disbelief, the priest adjourned the meeting.

Over the months that followed, different priests and nuns within the organization reached out to us—offering prayers, guidance, and insights. They knew the accused and were as appalled as we by their depraved actions. The collective kindness and support of these dedicated people helped us rebuild trust in the Catholic Church as a whole and in the goodness of the human spirit. The abusers were aberrations.

We lived within an hour of a large clinic that specialized in caring for abused children. I arranged for the initial evaluation and waited for Sarah while she met with a clinic psychiatrist and two social workers. Minutes became hours, and I grew apprehensive. Finally, she emerged, shaken by the recounting of events and the testing. According to the medical professionals, Sarah's victimization was one of the most psychologically sadistic that they had ever witnessed. Their report outlined her trauma in graphic terms, and they recommended that Sarah be kept on antianxiety medication while she processed her memories of the abuse.

Therapy was twice weekly, but during crisis times, when more memories surfaced, it increased as needed. Sarah fought going to the sessions. She felt so humiliated that she did not want to be in any situation that reminded her of the past. Because of Sarah's high resistance, the therapist worked with her on relaxation techniques, and then, as she slowly began to let go, the memories rushed forward and broke into her consciousness.

As they did, Sarah's nightmares became more intense. At times they engulfed her, and she became physically ill with nausea and asthma. She was unable to be around others during these crisis points and ended up missing over thirty days of school. Her grades tumbled.

I stayed home with Sarah when she wasn't at school. Often she could not sleep; the realistic nightmares—in which the abusers murdered Ron and me—provoked panic, and made her sob for me to hold her. She confided to the therapist that if I died, she would not be able to handle it and would want to die with me. She told the therapist that she would slash her wrists.

Slowly, more details emerged. In horror we learned that Sarah had gone into the seminary complex to see her father and had been beckoned by a priest to follow him into a nearby office. Another priest joined them and firmly held Sarah's hand to ensure that she would not run away. Sister Alice met them and took Sarah into her interior office, telling her that she was her godmother and that God wanted Sarah to come with her. They walked into the office, closed the door, and put Sarah on the desk, where they assaulted her. If Sarah cried, they threatened her. She disassociated and floated to the other side of the room.

Sarah described the priests in detail—their height, hair color, skin tone and freckles, and disposition. Initially she saw their faces as in a fog, because something was in front of the principal perpetrator's face. Once she identified the something as a camera, she could see their features clearly and was able to identify them in a photo lineup. We later learned that the ringleader had committed suicide the year before by jumping off a ship headed for Denmark. His suicide message stated that he was killing himself because he could not stop abusing children. He did not want to destroy another child's life. Since he had been moved from one assignment to another for sex offenses, no one was certain how many children he had traumatized.

Sarah was a victim of a child-pornography ring ensconced in the seminary. She described in terrorizing detail the threats she had endured. A knife was held to her ribs, and she was told that they would skin her alive if she talked. They warned her that they had already killed several other children who had spoken. They put large pornographic photographs of her on the table, warning that they would enlarge these photos and display them on the church altar if she said anything. Each time she moaned, they threatened to rape her mother, and they explicitly explained how they would do so. Then they claimed that they had already raped me because of her lack of cooperation, and added that my "cries could be heard for miles around." They also described how they were going to kill her father if she talked. And they stated repeatedly that God hated her and was throwing her into the pits of hell. They added that Mary, the mother of Jesus, hated her as well.

Within the confines of a seminary, and just a few yards from the chapel, Sarah was repeatedly and ritualistically abused by those who had dedicated themselves to sharing the Gospel message. Over the span of a year, she was threatened with distorted images of the Divine and nearly killed.

A tidal wave of sadness pounded me, crushing my chest until I could barely breathe. How could this have happened? How could people do such unspeakable things to an innocent child, *my* child? Caught in the swells of this storm, I was tossed and battered by hideous images and jolting questions. These perpetrators were Ron's colleagues; he worked with them every day. They used him to get to Sarah. But why?

Shortly before the abuse began, Ron had reported the ringleader priest to the seminary leadership. Stories were circulating about children being abused in the parishes at which this priest served. This information was corroborated by those who worked directly with the priest. Was Sarah the victim of retaliation? Could it be that abominable? Was her victimization a carefully orchestrated payback? While I was tortured by these questions and haunted by Sarah's experience, Ron was undaunted. "Let it go, Gwen; you need to move on," he'd say. "The past is past; we must focus on the present!"

But I couldn't forget about it. Held in the grip of despair night after night, I lay awake, searching my memories for any clue to understand what had occurred.

I remembered Sarah at five years old telling me that I only wanted to hurt her, that I hated her. At the time, I thought maybe she was jealous of her new baby brother. But now I understood differently. Sister Alice and the priests told Sarah over and over again that her parents wanted them to abuse her in order to help control her. They also told her that we hated her because every time she did not cooperate with them, they made us suffer. The pedophiles incarcerated Sarah in a deadly psychological prison.

I recalled how Sarah used to have a great love for "Mommy Mary" and Jesus, and then suddenly she recoiled from all images or mention of them. She had nightmares of being tossed into hell, of witches attacking her, of bad people killing her family members.

And she developed a terrible fear of nuns. I thought about how I shared this with a priest friend, and he assured me that this stage would pass.

I remembered with wrenching sadness a late-night emergency-room visit. Sarah could barely breathe because of her asthma. The doctor took her in right away and administered the first shot. She looked so frail on the hospital bed, her breathing labored and shallow. After the nurse administered the second shot, Sarah was still struggling for each breath, but she asked, "Mommy, why doesn't God love me?" I explained how God loved her very much, but she asked again, "But why does God make me have asthma?" Finally, she said, "Mommy, you look so tired. Won't you lie down here with me?" I explained that I was fine, and not to worry about me. If only I could go back to that moment now, I would lie down on the bed and hold my baby.

I remembered going to Sarah's kindergarten teacher to ask if everything was okay, because I was concerned about Sarah's comments and her nightmares. The teacher was reassuring, saying that a lot of kids went through this, and then explained that she had not noticed anything unusual.

I remembered taking the children to an international bazaar the nuns hosted. Sister Alice opened the door when we arrived, and looked down at Sarah and called her by name. I recalled being perplexed that she knew Sarah, but assumed it was because Sarah had met her when she visited her father at the seminary.

Then one morning I went through the photo albums and saw clearly what I had missed before: a happy, joyful child of four; a big-eyed, frightened child of five. I also went through a small collection of her early artwork, finding two drawings that the therapist confirmed were the results of her abuse—a child looking up to the heavens, pleading to be forgiven, and a man holding a dagger, with only a circle for a face.

Many nights Sarah slept with us; her nightmares and worries of reprisal left her unable to sleep. As she snuggled close, she whispered, "I've been so lonely, Mommy. I couldn't tell anyone about what happened, because they would come after me."

As I consoled her, I fell into the silence of my own pain. Is there any greater sorrow than that of a parent for a child who is suffering? One night Sarah asked me what was wrong, and I simply responded that I wished I had known what was happening; I would have done something. Sarah's words cut deeper than the pain.

"Mommy, I would feel so sad if you or Dad felt guilty for this. You are the best parents any child could ever have. I am so lucky I can talk to you about this now. Don't feel sad."

Months passed, and the hard work of recovery was evident. Sarah laughed more, she hung out with friends at school, and she resumed her dance classes. On one quiet afternoon, I asked if she could stay with her brothers while I went to a special workshop on healing that was offered to counselors and social workers. My hope was that I might learn something that could help the entire family. Sarah was fourteen years old, and she didn't mind staying with her younger brothers. I rented a children's video for them to watch and made popcorn for them to share. I left thinking that all was well, but it wasn't.

As the therapist led the group in a visualization meditation, I plainly heard these words: *Call home!* I might have ignored this message as just my usual anxiety, except for the fact that I heard it again, and more strongly this time: *CALL HOME!* I quickly got up and went over to the instructor's desk, where there was a phone. Friends in the group watched me carefully as I dialed my home. They came to my side when they heard my distress. Johnny answered the phone, crying.

"What's wrong, Johnny?" I asked.

"I don't know, Mommy. Sarah just keeps screaming," he replied.

"Let me talk with her, Johnny," I said.

"She's locked the door, Mommy; we can't get in," he cried.

"Let me talk with Andrew." Andrew took the phone and was also crying.

"What is happening?" I asked him.

"Can't you hear her, Mommy? She keeps yelling and won't stop," he explained.

"Go tell her she must come to the phone," I replied.

"She only yells at us to go away. She's locked in the bathroom," he sobbed.

I told Andrew how to open the door and then explained that I was giving the phone to my friend, and asked him to talk with her until I got home. My friend quickly took the phone and began comforting Andrew. He was still on the phone with my friend when I arrived. Johnny was beside him, still crying.

I opened the bathroom door to find Sarah curled up in the fetal position in the bathtub. She kept moaning, "They hurt me so bad, they hurt me so bad..." and then she would scream. I pulled her out of the tub, wrapped a towel around her stiff little body, and held her tight. Within a few minutes, the workshop teacher and two social workers arrived. The teacher helped me with Sarah, and each social worker held one of the boys. We talked quietly and prayed, until finally Sarah fell asleep. Pale-faced, the boys were in shock. It was the birth of another memory.

Once again, Sarah's therapy increased to several times a week. Her extreme anxiety was accompanied by the sensation of her throat closing. She felt as if she could not breathe, and at times she could not eat or drink. Her symptoms increased to the point that she started choking at school. So severe were her sensations that students tried to administer the Heimlich maneuver. Finally she remembered having been choked repeatedly.

Because of the extent of the abuse, the therapist stated that Sarah was fortunate to be alive. She further explained that Sarah braved this horror utterly alone, because the abusers had convinced her that she was a human sacrifice and no longer part of her family.

Sarah continued to ask me if I found her *gross*; she felt so ugly, so dirty, and so alone. I kept assuring her that she was incredibly courageous and utterly beautiful, but she would only sob inconsolably.

"I called for God," she would confess. "I asked for help, but He didn't help me. Why didn't He help me, Mommy?"

Her questions tore at my heart. How does a mother answer questions such as these when her own heart is grieving? A mother's tears meld with those of her child, until just a cavernous silence remains. There are no words in this place of crushing desolation. I could not pray. I could not hope. I was consumed by despair.

From this place of chilling abandonment, while staring numbly at the wooden planks in the floor, I said, "You know my heart, God, you know my heart." I was aware that the sun was shining outside, but I did not care; I could hear my children playing downstairs, but I was unmoved. I sat in a place of no light—in the heart of anguish.

It was then that I saw in my mind's eye a person with a shriveled arm. The arm looked pathetic, as it was rigid, withered, and unusable. As I studied this image, I heard, *What are you feeling as you look at him?* I realized that I felt pity and empathy.

Then I was shown a heart, the heart of one of the abusers. It was calcified; layer upon layer of hardened masses covered this fragile muscle. As I looked, I realized with a start that this person was incapable of experiencing love—either giving or receiving it. His heart, *their* hearts, were atrophied. And I felt pity for them. Such damaged people are dangerous and need to be permanently incarcerated. That said, because of this inner vision, I was able to perceive these sick people with an emotion other than just rage. I saw them as human beings greatly damaged, with the worst handicap of all—no ability to love. Strangely, this emotion of pity opened a door in my own heart, and I could again pray.

Over the next months and years, I searched for therapeutic ways to help release Sarah's sorrows. I took her to see multiple hands-on healers who worked with her energy field, massage therapists who helped her muscles relax, counselors who assisted her in reframing her experience. The tentacles of the abuse stretched deep within her cells, and she required the brilliance and patience of a diverse group of healing professionals.

Sarah's courage ultimately forged a healing pathway through the ashes of depravity, and her determination retrieved her childhood from the clutches of sordidness. Walking with her through this travail, I grew in my respect for and love of Mary, the mother of Jesus—for I had glimpsed her pain as I, too, stood at the foot of the cross.

The Decision

Sarah's struggle raked my heart, as surely as the moldboard plow my father used in the cotton fields as a boy. In the deep furrows of my anguish, sorrow found fertile ground. Ron was right to insist that I stop obsessing about what Sarah endured; tragedy bent my back as it did my spirit. "Let it go," he'd say in frustration. "You need to move on!" And though I didn't know how to "let it go," I knew that I needed to do so for my family and for me.

On a Sunday afternoon, while paging through the regional section of the *New York Times*, I noticed a job announcement for a newly created position at a Catholic university in Connecticut. Though I was quite content teaching at the small college near our home, this announcement sparked my interest. It was something new. I reread the announcement again and again. *Could this be an answer to my prayers?* I wondered.

Ron urged me to apply for the job. It would mean more security for the family, an easier commute for him, and better access to ballet training for Sarah. With both a degree in theology and a degree in counseling, I was academically qualified. I sent in my application, and in less than a month, I was invited for an interview. I had never heard of the college prior to reading the announcement, but I was intrigued by the possibility and the adventure.

Arriving early for the interviews, I strolled the sidewalks

crisscrossing the hills of this idyllic campus. As I paused by the pond and the pesky geese, I wondered what it would be like to work in one of the manor-style buildings. Everything was pristine, and everyone seemed so happy. *This will be a fresh beginning for our family*, I thought.

Throughout the long day, I answered questions, shared ideas, and spoke about my professional background and training with several assigned groups: managers, faculty, and students. When I left that day, I didn't know if I was perceived as a strong candidate or not, but a few weeks later I got a phone call from the vice president, asking me if I would accept the position. "Yes," I quickly responded, trying to control my excitement. He explained that my contract would be sent via FedEx and added that my start date would be one month later—April 1. My family and I were elated.

For three months, I drove back and forth to my new job, until our family found a place to live close to the university. My four hours of travel, two hours each way, began at five o'clock in the morning, to avoid the worst rush-hour traffic, and ended at six or seven in the evening. During my commute, I thought a lot about the children and about my marriage. Though I didn't like the drive itself, it nevertheless provided time to ponder.

Sitting in traffic, I observed men angrily bump their cars as they yelled at each other through open windows. I watched women wrestle with their pantyhose and then their makeup. I noticed drivers writing out their agendas or next novel. I saw people pound their dashboards and yell with fists in the air at the indignity of sitting still. I witnessed the world of dream chasers and empire builders, and I wondered, *Who am I?* As I watched my freeway comrades prepare for or despair their day, I realized that my unnamed traveling companions were probably looking at me in the same way. We were all nowhere going somewhere.

National Public Radio escorted me to and from my job and further enabled my itinerant contemplation. Between *Morning Edition* and *All Things Considered*, I reviewed my life and my circumstances.

One day, as I crossed the Throgs Neck Bridge, Senator Joe Biden was interviewed about his proposed Violence Against Women Act. He argued persuasively on behalf of battered women, and as he did so, I felt strangely exposed. When he described the prevalence of domestic violence, though, I was taken aback. There were others, many others like me, hiding in the shadows of life, and I had been unaware. My no-name sisters knew fear like I knew it, and they probably rationalized the violence, as I did. *It's not so bad*, I would think. *After all, it's not every day.*

With flashes of Ron's hands clutching my neck, of his twisting my arms and grabbing my breasts, of his shoving me against the walls in each of the places we had called home, with these images and more, I drove home. The physical violence was more sporadic now that I was gone so much of the day. There was less time for escalation. The verbal abuse, however, was unrelenting. I could not do anything right.

Ron had removed his wedding ring before I began commuting to the university. He said it interfered with his work in the city. When I discovered receipts for dinners and hotels and learned that his evening obligations were not all work related, I didn't feel hurt by the infidelities—I felt diminished by the fact that I wasn't worth a dinner or hotel suite. I realized that Ron had made a decision about our marriage, whether he voiced it or not. And as I drove through traffic jams and daunting weather, I made mine. I did not know when or how it would happen, but I knew that divorce was inevitable. Ron and I had effectively separated; we had silently and definitively chosen to end our lengthy marriage. At some point in time, we would acknowledge our decision out loud to each other—but until then, we would continue our charade.

After work one evening, a friend stopped by to see me. "You are too stressed out!" she insisted. "You spend the workweek on the road or in your office. You need to relax!" She convincingly explained that I should have a massage and then handed me a gift certificate, knowing full well that it would obligate me to go. So, on a Saturday afternoon, I grudgingly put on my sweats and headed to the spa.

"Is this your first massage?" the therapist asked, as I stood awkwardly in the dimly lit room, not knowing what to do. Anticipating my response, she patiently explained the process and asked that I undress to my level of comfort.

"I'll begin with your back, so please lie facedown when you're ready," she instructed. "I'll be back in a minute."

I dutifully piled up my clothes on a corner chair and crawled under the sheet on the massage table. Enya's *Watermark* played quietly in the background as I squirmed to get comfortable.

"Do you have any problems I should know about?" the therapist asked when she returned.

"Problems? Umm, not really," I responded, wondering if I should tell her about my sore neck or my tender feet. I had no idea what I should say or not.

As I lay on my stomach, breathing deeply the scent of lavender oil, the therapist began rhythmically moving up my back. I was starting to relax, when she pressed a tender area in my upper back. Anxiety caught me off-guard, and I began to cry. I tried not to, but my back pain weakened my resolve, and tears fell through the face cradle to the floor below. *What is happening to me?* I wondered. Too embarrassed to speak, I said nothing. But the therapist noticed my discomfort and whispered, "Take a deep breath. Now another, and another…and release." The massage was not painful, but the area she touched was raw with grief.

She then held my right arm and started rubbing my triceps. "Let your arm drop into my hand," she said softly. She repeated her request again and reminded me to relax. Then she stopped altogether. Still holding my arm, she whispered into my ear.

"You are in an abusive relationship, aren't you?" she said.

"Why do you ask?" I responded, taken aback by her comment.

"Your muscles are locked in a terror state," she answered caringly.

"I—I don't understand," I stammered, not sure what I should reveal.

"Don't worry," she said, "your muscles will respond to gentleness."

I left the spa confused by what had occurred. I had held my secret for more than twenty years, but within an hour it had been bared to someone who had simply touched my muscles. How could this be? For about fifteen minutes, I sat in my car, pondering what lay ahead. I was both curious and anxious; I knew I was on the verge of notable change. Driving home, I decided to make another appointment. I wanted to better understand what had occurred.

I arrived early for the second massage. I was ready this time; I knew what to expect. Just as before, I lay facedown on the table and awaited the therapist. She again started with my back, and again my back belied my confidence, and I started to cry. The therapist helped me breathe through the sadness and explained how the body absorbs the pain we suppress and stores the memories within our cells.

"When we are touched," she said tenderly, "these emotions and memories can enter our consciousness."

"But will they ever leave?" I asked.

"With time and patience, they will," she responded.

During one session shortly thereafter, the therapist wiped away tears of her own. As I lay on my back with a small flaxseed pillow over my eyes, she put her hands under my shoulders, massaging tender points. Sniffling, she finally paused to get a tissue. "I'm sorry," she said. "I feel so much sadness when I rub these areas."

At the close of our session, the therapist suggested that I read about the relationship between our emotions and our body. She gave me a small blue book by Louise Hay, *Heal Your Body*. "This has helped me with my struggles," she said. "I think it will help you as well."

I read the book in one sitting and had a better sense of how our thoughts and emotions affect our well-being. We were created to be whole, to be balanced, but our response to the stresses of life can interfere with our ability to be healthy, depending on our self-talk. I learned that the upper back is associated with feeling loved or emotionally supported, and the shoulders carry the challenges of life. I understood my tears during the massage and honored my body for its efforts to shelter me. I also crafted affirmations based on Hay's model, and I began saying them throughout the day. "I love and approve of myself," I'd mutter. "I love and approve of myself. I am supported by life. I choose joy." It seemed artificial at first, but then the words came naturally.

My job at the university was demanding. I oversaw several large departments and also met with students and parents regularly. The opening of the academic year was particularly challenging. Because of the nature of my obligations, I asked Ron not to invite anyone to our home during the first three days of school, when my responsibilities were most intense. He worked at a global firm in New York City and frequently wined and dined international guests in our house, but I did not want his business associates dropping by during a time when I was unable to serve them. On this occasion, though, Ron did not heed my request. On the first day of school, as I was greeting thousands of students and parents at the university, Japanese visitors arrived at our home.

In most cultures, but certainly in Asian cultures, it is assumed that the wife will serve the guests. The best I could do was drive from work to the house for a few minutes at a time. I could not be both places at once, yet it was essential that I be at the university and expected that I be home for Ron and his guests. It was an impossible situation. I did not meet anyone's expectations that day, and this failure resulted in arguments and threats as soon as the visitors left. Nothing upset Ron more than appearing poorly to others.

"Who do you think you are?" Ron said as he pushed me backward. "You made me look like a fool."

"I told you I had to be at the university," I responded quickly. "I had no choice!"

"Why? Did you give directions to wayward freshmen? Huh? What was so important that you couldn't be here?" he taunted.

"I had to speak to the entire freshman class and separately with their parents," I said, growing even more anxious.

"Really," he mocked. "What's the real reason, Gwen?" He pushed me farther into the bedroom.

"That *is* the reason," I explained. "It's my job to be there for the opening."

"Admit it: you weren't here because you wanted to make me look bad! Admit it, bitch!" he demanded.

There was nothing more I could say. Ron believed I had intentionally plotted to make him look bad. When I went to bed that evening, I was aware that my entire body was rigid. I was very frightened. I did not know what was going to happen next. And then I recalled what the massage therapist had said: "Your muscles are locked in a terror state." She was right.

The university became a safe haven for me. I was respected, validated, and supported. The intercity program I created garnered notable statewide attention. Our cross-cultural program became a cornerstone for addressing diversity concerns. Universities across the country began to use elements of the first-year-experience program that I established. The environment itself, despite its challenges, was healing. During this time, Ron was rarely home, because he traveled internationally much of the year. I was responsible for the house and the children. One day, the director of the university's health center said to me, "The only reason you are still married to Ron is that he is usually gone." I thought about her comment momentarily and then acknowledged that she was probably right. The university was my lifeline, but it could not fix the marriage, nor could I ignore the decision to divorce much longer.

I enrolled in a nine-month experiential retreat that was structured for lay people who were working. Called the Spiritual Exercises in Everyday Life, it offered an approach to prayer and scriptural reflection that anyone could use. Each week I met with a spiritual director, a Jesuit priest, to review my experience with prayer and with the assigned biblical readings. He read my journal and gently guided me to see what might be interfering with my ability to feel

God's love. We always began with prayer, followed by my reflections on the readings.

"Your soul is like a Japanese garden," Father Simon would say. "We need to approach it with awe and gentleness. Tell me about your readings and what you learned this week."

"I meditated on the woman afflicted with a lengthy ailment," I responded. "My heart went out to her, and then I realized that I saw myself as this woman," I added, as I handed him my journal entry.

Luke 13:10–17

Not only did I feel sad reading about the woman, I strongly identified. She was bent over because Satan… "bound her for eighteen long years." My whole body felt constricted with pain. Jesus called me to him and put his hands on my head, and told me he was removing the binds one at a time that I might know the impact of sin.

I never realized how much pain my body carried. When I was in my thirties, I had no sense of my body. I was not in my body. Now I'm finding myself in my body and knowing incredible pain. It's been a long absence that has left my body scarred.

Jesus said to me, "My child, come to me. As I loosen the binds, you know the pain that has numbed your heart for years, but this pain is being released; it is not being inflicted. It is joy that awaits you—joy that knows no bounds. I am guiding you each step of the way."

After reading the entry, Father Simon commented on the tender love of God and then asked a few pointed questions.

"In your reflection, you've recounted how the pain is being healed, but you've also mentioned that it has left you scarred. Can you explain that for me, please?" he asked.

"I'm not sure," I said, thinking about the meditation. "I suppose I felt that it was permanent—the damage from the pain."

"And yet, in your conversation with Jesus, you are told that the pain is being released. Do you think he is referring to part of it or all of it?" he inquired.

I thought about his question for a moment and then responded, "I think he was referring to all of it."

"So, let's pause a minute. What is going on in your heart that makes you think you are scarred for life by pain?" he asked thoughtfully.

As I considered how to answer him, I started to cry. He offered me a tissue and waited for me to compose myself.

"I don't know," I said. "It just seems like there has been too much."

"Too much for God or too much for you?" he asked. "You've written, 'This pain is being released; it is not being inflicted. It is joy that awaits you—joy that knows no bounds.' What does this mean to you?"

"The pain I have known is being released, and in its stead will be joy," I said.

"Exactly," he said excitedly. "That was the promise—*joy*, not pain."

"I understand now," I said, smiling.

Our weekly sessions were both revelatory and hilarious. One time, we crossed the campus grounds to his office.

"We're not walking on the sidewalk today," he said, climbing the grass embankment.

I felt uncomfortable walking on the grass. We had signs up—I had helped put them there—asking students to use the sidewalks. I just couldn't walk on the grass.

"Come on," he insisted. "Today you're going to do something you're not supposed to do. Let's see if the world comes to an end."

"Okay, but I don't like it!" I said, and he laughed heartily.

"Now, I want you to say, 'Fuck you!'"

"I can't say that," I protested.

"Sure you can," he asserted. "It's simple, just two words. Fuck you!" he said loudly.

"I just can't say it," I persisted.

"Let's try it another way. Fuck you, Ron! Try that!" Again, he laughed wholeheartedly.

This exercise went on for a while, until I finally gave in. He was unrelenting. When the words came out of my mouth, he raised his arms and shouted, "Alleluia!" Then we *both* laughed.

Father Simon helped me delve deeper into my interpretations of scripture and of the divine. His approach might have been unconventional at times, but it was effective. For this reason, the retreat itself was transformative. I was consistently met with compassion, and my insights were validated. Because of the trust that developed, for the first time I spoke of domestic violence. To my surprise, Father Simon was already aware, but he had waited for me to feel safe enough to share it. Over the next months, when I was caught in the throes of confusion or fear, he helped me step back and breathe. The retreat process itself became a sanctuary for change.

That June, Nicole Brown Simpson was killed, and every TV network reported the tragedy. I was riveted. As I sat alone watching the news one night, the reporter introduced a psychologist who talked about the signs of domestic abuse as a list was projected on the screen. While I was reading these indicators, an awful sense of dread came over me, and I froze. Every sign—*every one*, from the belittling, controlling behavior and constant blame to the threats and actual use of violence—I experienced personally with some regularity. I felt as if I were tumbling through space without anything firm to hold on to. How could it be that I hadn't seen this clearly before?

After my months of scriptural reflection, the amnesiac blankets that covered my pain fell away. Now that I could feel again, every criticism from Ron, every threat, the harshness of his words and his behavior, seared my heart. The retreat process had brought the clarity that was needed, and I knew it was time to take active steps to divorce Ron. Nevertheless, the realization that it was crucial to take those steps was petrifying. I could no longer remain in a relationship that did damage to my very person, but I was afraid. I was afraid of what people might say, afraid of not being accepted by the church, afraid of not being able to support myself and the children.

Because of my distress, I decided to visit my spiritual director from many years prior, a cloistered nun in upstate New York. The casual wanderer would not know that down a country road, just beyond a forest of tall oak trees, women are quietly at prayer. Most drive past the area unaware that they have skirted holy ground. I knew about the cloister and Sister Grace only through a friend.

"People come from all over the world to see her," my friend had explained. "She can see into your soul."

"What do you mean, 'she can see into your soul'?" I asked, feeling uncomfortable.

"You'll find out if she agrees to meet with you," she responded. "It's hard to explain."

It had been a decade since I had last met with Sister Grace, but when she greeted me at the door, clasping my hands warmly as she had always done, the years faded away. She led me to an interior meeting room, invited me to have a seat, and then sat opposite me.

"It's so good to see you, Gwen. Tell me how you are doing," she said in her characteristically subdued voice. I talked about the children, about moving to Connecticut, and about my new job, but she stopped me and asked again, "How are *you* doing, Gwen?" She watched me intently as I stammered and tried to find words. "Why did you come to see me?" she asked, as if to help me with my ramblings.

"Sister Grace, things are not good between Ron and me. It's been that way for a very long time," I explained. "He is verbally and physically abusive, and I've come to seek your advice about what I should do."

"What advice are you needing, Gwen? I think you know what to do," she responded.

"Perhaps, but I need to be sure. I just completed a lengthy retreat, and through that process I realized that I cannot endure the violence anymore. But I'm afraid to take the steps I need to take to end the violence. And I worry about the children," I said.

"And by 'end the violence,' you mean divorce?" Sister Grace asked.

"Yes, divorce. I don't think there is any other way," I replied.

Never one to mince words, Sister Grace responded with only one sentence: "Gwen, if you do not divorce Ron, a greater divorce is going to happen in your soul."

In that defining moment, I saw my choice as an ultimatum.

"But...but what if I'm wrong? What if it's a mistake? What if I can't make it on my own?"

"Fear is not a reason to avoid doing what you need to do," she said simply.

"But...I feel like a failure," I said, ashamed of the words as soon as I spoke them.

"If you remain with him," she stated, "you will lose touch with the life and the joy you have come to know through the retreat." Then she added, "If you don't take this step, Gwen, your heart will once again become a grieving shell."

"I know what you are saying is true, because that is what my heart is saying as well. It's just that I was hoping for a simpler solution," I responded tearfully.

Sister Grace put her hand on mine and, looking directly into my eyes, said, "Let go, Gwen—only love awaits you."

For much of the hour-and-a-half drive home, I was in a state of shock. Though intellectually aware that I needed to file for divorce, I had somehow assumed that this saintly nun would miraculously make it all better. Instead, not only had she told me that I must divorce Ron, but she had also warned me about the consequences of *not* doing so. I had spent years running from my fear, and now I had a choice: my fear or my soul. If it hadn't been clear before this meeting, it certainly was now. I held on to the hope her final words had stirred: *only love awaits you.*

Almost as a confirmation of what I had learned, I had to deal with Ron's anger shortly after I got home. I was carrying soiled clothes downstairs to the basement, when Ron began yelling at me. He got threateningly close to me midway down the stairs. Andrew unexpectedly appeared at the foot of the stairs. Though I was relieved that he was there, because Ron would not touch me when the children were present, I was also embarrassed. Ron saw him and left. Andrew came up the stairs and with agitation said, "If any guy did this to one of the girls at my school, she would lay him out!" He then went outside.

Though just a child, Andrew let me know that such behavior was unacceptable, and that I should not allow it. His words weighed heavily upon me, and I felt my own failure for not acting sooner. In that moment, I also realized that Andrew often was around when Ron got angry. *Did he know?* I wondered. *Was he trying to protect me by being within sight?* I realized, just as Sister Grace had explained, I needed to confront my fear and act. My children shouldn't have to do that for me.

Over the next weeks and months, I sought the advice of women at the university who had gone through a divorce. They were all supportive, but they were also cautious with their suggestions. They warned me of the difficulties that lay ahead, explained the process for securing a restraining order, and outlined the financial steps I should take. Slowly I became aware of a whole network of women who had valiantly fought for their dignity. Importantly, I also began meeting with a counselor.

This was not the first counselor I had met with, but she was the first one I met with after I decided to divorce Ron. The prior counselors had all recommended divorce, but when they had done so, I had stopped therapy, feeling that I had somehow betrayed Ron. It was different this time, because I was ready to address my situation. Curiously, the first session began with an exploration of my interests and expectations.

"What do you like to do?" she asked. "What makes you happy?"

I hadn't expected these questions, and I sat there perplexed about what to say. Finally, I responded falteringly.

"My children make me happy," I said.

"Of course they do," the counselor retorted, "but I'm not talking about your children. I'm asking you what makes *you* happy."

"I don't understand," I said, very confused.

"Do you like to sing, dance, paint, scrapbook, travel, hike? What brings you joy?" she pressed.

Befuddled, I sat staring at her. I had never thought about what I liked or what made me happy. I searched my heart and my mind, but I could find nothing, nothing at all.

Slowly, one step at a time, through a combined counseling approach using artwork as well as ancient images and stories, I began to identify with women of strength and incidences of wholesomeness. My first drawing assignment was to symbolically sketch my life. I drew a small orange box within a larger black box. My written explanation was:

The small box in the center is the box Ron created and I accepted. It is well defined and sometimes comfortable. If I do what is expected, if I agree with him and am cordial, all is fine. But there's not much life in this box. I am mostly alone.

When I come out of this small box, I'm in another one. It's a bigger box, darker, filled with voices that say, You've made a mistake, you're a failure, you can't make it, you'll fall apart, you'll be alone—really alone—you'll go crazy. It is a box of fear. I feel this fear physically: my body tightens, my stomach feels sick, and all my focus goes to watching/feeling these sensations, as though I have no control over them. This box terrifies me, so I stay close to the smaller box (the box that Ron created), because if I need to, I can go back in and feel safe because life is controlled in that box, everything is in its place. I am in my place. I know what I can do and cannot do.

Sometimes I go out of all the boxes, into the light. I'm not quite sure how I do this, or how I avoid the black box, but I do—sometimes. I leave and my spirit soars. I climb high into the heavens. I dance in the breeze. I feel free. When I am in this place, there is no fear, no darkness—only light and love.

It is my box, the large dark one, that keeps me from the light, that keeps me from joy and peace of mind. If I can dissolve this box, then I could leave the smaller one, because I wouldn't need it anymore.

The counselor worked with me to develop the skills needed to escape the imaginary boxes. I told her that I never wanted to repeat this life lesson again. I asked for her help in addressing all the ways in which I was entangled in self-defeating patterns. I was determined to leave the marriage a whole person.

Through the help of a friend, I met with an attorney, a kindly woman much older than I, and began taking steps to end the marriage. She helped me secure restraining orders to protect the family. Ron was served, and he went to live with his sister about twenty miles away. He also hired a female attorney, one of the best divorce attorneys in the greater New York area. It was an unfair match. I tried to prepare my attorney for what lay ahead, but in the end, I prepared myself.

At the initial court review, Ron's attorney argued for and got approval for required couples' therapy for the two of us and the right for Ron to live in our home until the divorce was final. I was speechless. Ron told the judge that he was brokenhearted and claimed that he had tried to get me into therapy for many years, but that I had always refused. In actuality, the opposite was true. He also stated that he had nowhere to live, even though he was staying with his sister a short distance away and an even shorter commute to his work. He pleaded to stay in our furnished walkout basement, promising that he would never come upstairs where I would be. He convincingly portrayed himself as misunderstood, dejected, and unjustly accused. It was quite the theatrical performance.

Shortly thereafter, Ron and I met with a court-approved social worker. He was a respected therapist who had considerable background working with estranged couples through the court. Our first session began as most do, with introductions and expectations, and then everything changed dramatically.

The social worker questioned each of us and countered some of Ron's comments with more questions. Ron became quite agitated with the therapist and pressed his points. The exchange escalated and got loud. I thought there was going to be a physical altercation, because both men were leaning forward and their tone was threatening. I moved my chair back out of the way. Then the therapist abruptly stopped the session.

Our second session began with the social worker's assessment that he had no hope for our marriage. He concluded by stating that he would not meet with us again, because he felt threatened by Ron and was worried for his own safety. We got up to leave, and Ron snapped at me that I had caused the problem.

We then met with a female counselor. She saw us individually and together. Ron claimed I had gotten too independent working at the college; he said he had tried to save the marriage but I was unwilling to cooperate. He added that he just could not understand me. As always, everything was my fault.

After a few sessions, the counselor spoke with me privately and confided that the results of her tests and conversations with Ron indicated that there was no hope for our marriage. She was very troubled by his behavior, and in particular by his lack of remorse. She was also concerned about my safety. She recommended a few books that she thought might illuminate the dynamics I had known in the marriage.

During the time when we met with the court-approved therapist, Ron lived downstairs—per the court. He had promised that he would never come upstairs, but he did. He ransacked my dresser, throwing clothes every which way. The only thing that was different about our living arrangement was that we did not share the master bedroom; otherwise, he used all the rooms in the house at will. The situation was untenable, and I let my attorney know that if anything happened to me, the State of Connecticut should be held responsible. I did not want to be a statistic, like so many women who file protective orders. That almost became a reality.

One of the requirements of the court order was, "The parties shall refrain from communicating with each other in any way, including any physical contact." Ron interpreted this mandate loosely. He would lounge in the family room and taunt me about what I was going to do about it. As I was bringing in the groceries one day, he accosted me. He got within two inches of my face and started yelling profanities and then said, "Come on, push me! Try it—hit me, nigger! Do it! You know you want to!" He was crazed with anger.

At that moment, I did not care what the consequences might be, I did not care if I died—I was determined to stand my ground. Glaring back at him, I shouted, "Get away from me!" And, to my surprise, he did.

Ron's attorney insisted on a deposition. She began with a litany of questions, but after an hour or more of this interrogation, she stopped and said, "What would it take to settle this?"

I realized at that moment that she knew I was a formidable witness. I told her simply, "I want a divorce, shared custody of the children, and our assets divided equally."

"That's all?" she snapped. "You don't want alimony?" I acknowledged that I did not.

As anyone who has gone through these steps can attest, the process is a solitary one. For women in abusive relationships, the process is assaultive. I managed my fear by focusing on the immediate situation. I pushed myself beyond my imagined limits. I wouldn't allow myself to cry, for I felt that my tears might engulf me, such that I would not be able to stop.

One evening, as I lay in the pain of my circumstances, I suddenly had a strong impression of Mary, the mother of Jesus, standing next to my bed. She was large and strong in stature, and did not look like the paintings of her as a young adolescent. Scriptural stories came to mind: of the wedding at Cana, and Mary telling Jesus more wine was needed; and of Mary by the cross, unintimidated by the yelling crowds or the soldiers who shoved her. The images were empowering, because they were images of strength, determination, and confidence. Over the months that followed, I summoned those qualities as I dealt with arguing attorneys, accusations from Ron's family, the embarrassment of telling certain colleagues at work, and so much more. I found the strength I desired and realized even more was available to me.

When we finally went to court, a friend from the university came with me. Before the judge arrived, Ron's attorney came over and loudly demanded my wedding ring, the stone of which had come from a pendant belonging to Ron's mother. I told her that I did not have it. She then repeatedly insisted that I tell her where it was. My attorney murmured, "You don't have to give it to her." But Ron's attorney was unswayed. Bemused by the drama unfolding in front of us, my friend smiled at me and said loudly, "Who does this bitch think she is?" Her statement and facial expression made me laugh, and I let go of my anxiety. Then the judge walked in and Ron's attorney quickly returned to the other side of the courtroom. I hadn't told Ron's attorney where the ring was because I was protecting my daughter. The day I had filed for divorce, I had given her the ring.

The divorce hearing was relatively brief, because we had reached an agreement to divide everything equally. This was a simple task, since we did not have much to divide. The house would be sold as quickly as possible, and I would stay there until the sale was finalized. The proceeds from the sale would be divided in half. The children would live with me, and Ron would help to support them financially until they reached eighteen years of age. When the judge realized that an agreement had been reached, he questioned me about my understanding and my willingness to accept the terms of the agreement. He also wanted to know who would be covering the children's insurance. I quickly said I would do so. Ron spoke up at one point during the hearing to say that I had been given too much, but the entire courtroom moaned, and Ron's attorney silenced him. The judge then declared the marriage null and void and, at the request of the two attorneys, ordered that the records be sealed. As we walked out of the courtroom, Ron scowled at me and said, "Well, you got what you wanted. Now we'll see if you can make it on your own!"

Twenty-five years to the day after I married Ron, I divorced him. The hearing had been set for a different day, but because of a calendar problem at the court, the date was changed. When my attorney realized that it was our anniversary, she did not want to proceed, explaining that she had never divorced a couple on their twenty-fifth anniversary. From my vantage point, it made perfect sense. Alpha and omega: the beginning and the end.

Even after the divorce was finalized, only my closest friends and confidents understood the reasons for our split. I thought it best to remain silent for the children's sake, and so I did. On one occasion, however, Ron's sister called, yelling at me. She accused me of overreacting to his infidelity, to being selfish, and to being cruel. I finally stopped her and asked, "Do you want me to tell the truth? Do you want me to tell your mother about her son and what occurred behind closed doors? Do you want me to explain the violence?" She stopped her tirade, slammed down the phone, and never called again.

Domestic violence is usually not reported, and this fact is often misunderstood. Certainly, victims do not report the violence because of the very real possibility of retaliation, but there is a deeper reason for their silence. To report partner violence is to betray the partner, it is to forsake the dream of a happily-ever-after marriage, it is to contend with the real and imaginary voices of condemnation, and it is to destroy the family unit.

When we first fall in love with our partner, we also fall in love with a vision of happiness. That vision is the lens through which we judge ourselves. It is integrally linked to our sense of self. To expose our partner is to expose our perceived failure. For that reason, victims will pretend that all is well until they cannot pretend any longer.

When I saw my internist after an incident, he got very frustrated with me and said, "Why do you put up with this crap, Gwen? You're an intelligent woman; you're a professional. You don't need to stay in this marriage!" His choice of words belied his premise—that only the less intelligent or uneducated are in abusive relationships. But, truthfully, domestic violence is indiscriminate. The rich and the poor, the black and the white, the educated and the uneducated—all are equally vulnerable.

One day, a student came to see me on behalf of her roommate. She explained that her friend's body was covered with bruises and stated that she had photos that substantiated her claim. According to the student, her roommate's boyfriend beat her roommate regularly. She pleaded with me to intervene. I asked her to invite the student to come see me, and she did.

Mary walked into my office timidly. Her big blue eyes were red-rimmed; her long blond hair draped over her full-length coat. Looking vacantly out my office window, she dismissed her roommate's concerns and explained that her boyfriend loved her. I asked if I could meet him, and she agreed. The following week, both sat in front of me.

I shared that some concern had been raised about whether their relationship was a healthy one. The boyfriend was incredulous, demanding to know who could have made such a complaint. Before I could respond, Mary spoke up, tearfully defending her boyfriend. She maintained that he loved her and never hurt her. I explained that it is normal protocol to follow up when concerns are raised, and I certainly was not making an accusation. In their case, I said, it was clear that they both loved each other.

"It refreshes me when I see real love," I explained. "Too often, I have to deal with weakness, impotence."

"What do you mean?" the boyfriend asked, glaring at me. I clearly had his attention.

"Well, only the weak use control and violence to exert power," I responded. "As pitiful as that is, it is the truth."

"I don't use violence!" he stated emphatically as he moved to the edge of his chair.

"Oh, I know you don't," I responded. "Mary just told me that you don't. I was talking about other cases I manage with boyfriends who are violent. They are the ones who are pitiful."

Over the next thirty minutes or so, I described situations of dating violence and intentionally used *weakness* and *impotence* interchangeably. At the end of the discussion, I thanked them for loving each other as they did.

The following week, the roommate stopped by my office to let me know that Mary and her boyfriend had broken up.

More recently, I was in a local grocery store, when I heard a man berating his wife. He called her stupid and said she would never learn, as she picked up one vegetable after another and deftly put them into the basket. When I looked over at her, I saw myself. She smiled as her husband put her down, she smiled when he told her she was a fool, and she just kept shopping as though she did not hear his comments. I so wanted to tell her husband what I thought of him, but I knew that she—not I—would pay the price for my indulgence. I also wanted to speak with the woman directly, but I realized that anything I might say would not be received. She was not ready yet to give up her dream. Her decision was still to come.

Recovering Joy

My friend has a poster with a quote from C. S. Lewis hanging in a very visible location in her office. It reads: "Crying is all right in its own way while it lasts. But you have to stop sooner or later, and then you still have to decide what to do."

"It's a reminder," Mary told me, pointing to her sign, "that I can cry, scream, even curse at my circumstance, but in the end, I need to decide how I am going to proceed."

"So, are you trying to tell me something?" I asked teasingly.

"You?" she replied, with a hugely mischievous smile. "Of course not—I'm talking about myself."

"I doubt that," I said, returning her smile, "but the fact is, it is time to move forward."

Throughout my life, I've hoped for a miracle that would erase the past and sketch another present. Imagining myself to be another Gulliver, pinned down by real and imaginary forces, I'd think, *I'm scared, poor me,* or some variant of that theme, while I pleaded for divine intervention. What I often did not see at those life junctures was that the universe itself was waiting on me, and what held me captive was ultimately me. I was and am, you were and are, surrounded by miracles. Some of these miracles take our breath away; others quietly help us grapple with our circumstance and choose our way.

My Jesuit spiritual director had made me shout a profanity at the injustices of life. As crazy as I thought his prompting to be, I now understand that he was trying to help me own my buried fury. Who doesn't want to lash out at the person who has hurt her child? Who doesn't want to fight back when attacked? It is innate to want justice, and deep down we want the offender to suffer like we suffer. But "sooner or later…you still have to decide what to do." My spiritual director's approach might have been unconventional, but he helped me realize that within my rage was the strength I needed to find joy.

The baby photo I had shared at the workshop on healing years before was of the toddler me sitting in front of a small Christmas tree holding my new dolly and smiling happily. "What happened between then and now?" the facilitators had asked me, noting that I no longer had that same smile. I couldn't answer their question at the time, but if they were to ask me now, I would respond, "Life happened, and I managed as best I could."

Through struggles, some severe and some unrelenting, we are all pushed to the edge of our understanding. Clinging to the rim of that precipice, we are often unaware that it is a threshold. What feels like death may be a beginning. We do our best in the moment; sometimes we hide, and sometimes we act boldly. Either way, we respond, handicapped by personal history and circumstance. As unbelievable as it may seem at the time, when tragedy touches us, it is we who decide our way.

Sarah and I had both lost a sense of who we were through our independent but commingled life struggles. In Sarah's young heart, she concluded that God did not love her; in my adult heart, I thought my suffering was deserved and redemptive. Not only were our conclusions faulty, they were destructive. When we imagine ourselves as separated from the source of all love, a chorus of judging voices erupts: *You are bad. You are a failure. It would be better if you weren't alive. No one likes you. You are ugly. You are crazy. You are not worth anything.* Under such attack, we can be so immobilized by fear that we become living mannequins, mechanically going through the motions of life. Where love and hope should dwell, shame and guilt take residence. If this occurs, it is not enough to hear, "God loves you," even though it is true. Logic itself cannot restore us to a place of joy; we need the direct experience of love.

For more than two decades I had tried to shield my children from the sorrows in our home, but I now realize that my secret separated me from them. My closeted life held my heart, with its forgotten dreams and innocent longings—a heart that the healers had described as "shattered in little pieces" and "held together with tape and string." Though I did not know how to bridge the years of hiding, I knew I needed to bring levity into our home and healing into our lives.

Every day I drove past St. Charles parish on my way to and from work. Its tall white columns seemed forbidding to me, but it was this church that opened its doors to us. The marquee by the road announced a healing Mass and included the words ALL ARE WELCOME. It didn't say ONLY THOSE WHO ATTEND THE CHURCH, or ONLY THOSE WHO BELIEVE AS WE BELIEVE—it just said ALL ARE WELCOME. I told Sarah about the event; she thought about it a while and then said she wanted to attend.

So, on the day of the service, Sarah, Andrew, Johnny, and I headed to the church with more than a little trepidation. As we walked toward the steps leading to the tall wooden doors, which were now open wide, Sarah stopped, and we stopped with her. She was having second thoughts about going in.

"Shall we go in the side door?" I asked. She looked up at me and nodded, and the boys followed as we led the way. People were congregated toward the front of the church; we sat near the back, where no one would notice us.

"Good morning," the priest said when he walked to the front of the altar. "Today we gather to ask the Holy Spirit to anoint our hearts with joy and restore our bodies to full health that we might be whole and complete." He introduced the visiting ministers and then brought everyone into prayer. Over the next hour or more, the congregation focused on healing through prayer and song.

Sarah did not move or speak throughout the entire service. She stared straight ahead as though she were in a catatonic state. "Sarah," I asked, "is everything okay?" There was no response. "Sarah, would you like to go home?" Again, no response. She did not even acknowledge that she heard me. While focused on Sarah, Johnny escaped my hold and playfully crawled under the pews, randomly popping up like a prairie dog to see where we were. He crossed the aisles and maneuvered through legs and feet, to both my dismay and amusement. My attempts to get him to return to his seat only spurred him on, so I let him be. Andrew sat silently next to me, watching everything.

At the end of the service, the priest announced that anyone who wanted individual prayer could come forward and meet with one of the visiting healers.

"We can leave now," I said to Sarah. "The Mass is over."

"No, I want to go up there!" she said firmly, still staring straight ahead. And, without another word, she stood and marched determinedly to the front of the church.

I quickly turned to the boys.

"Mommy's going up to the altar with Sarah," I said. "Just wait here, okay?"

"No, I want to go too!" they said in unison as they crawled over me to follow their sister.

Everything was happening so fast. I hurried to catch up with my children, and reached the altar as a minister extended her hands over Sarah's head. She immediately fell back and was gently guided to the floor by another minister. I stared in amazement as softness moved across her beautiful face while she lay peacefully on the floor. Andrew was next. The minister held her hands above his head, and, just like Sarah, Andrew fell back and was caught by another minister, who guided him to the floor, where he now lay serenely.

"Are these your children?" the minister asked, smiling.

"Yes, they are," I acknowledged.

"You are very blessed," she said, and, seeing Johnny in front of her, she asked, "Can I pick him up and hold him? He is so small."

"Of course, please do," I responded.

She picked Johnny up, and, while holding him in her arms, she prayed. My once-active child immediately became a limp doll, sleeping soundly.

With my three children lying silently before me, I asked for prayers. I was conflicted about doing so, because I was not sure what was happening, but I finally took the leap. The minister placed her hands lightly on my head. I tried to resist the swaying that I felt, but then a soft wind passed by and I fell back as well, into the arms of a waiting minister.

As we walked home, the children were gleeful and excitedly shared their experience.

"Did you feel the wind?" they asked one another.

"I could hear it as it approached," Sarah said. "And then I felt love go through my body. Did you feel that too?"

"I felt it too," I explained. "The peace was wonderful, wasn't it?"

The boys were so happy that they were giddy, and Johnny wanted to go back for more.

As I watched them tease one another, I realized that a fragile bridge had been built between all things related to church and our lives.

On another occasion, the weather forecasters had predicted snow, but they had not prepared us for a blizzard. Once nine inches had accumulated on the ground, businesses and schools began closing early. Johnny's teacher called to ask me to come pick him up as soon as possible. I got there at the same time as many other parents. It was a mess: cars were stalled in the streets while snowplows tried to clear the way. Our old Dodge Dart grumbled and slipped side to side; the driving conditions were worsening by the moment.

I buckled Johnny into the car and told him, somewhat in jest, that we ought to pray to get home safely. I could not see the road ahead, our wipers were working only randomly, and I was alarmed. My nervousness made Johnny anxious as well.

"I'm scared, Mommy," he sobbed.

"We'll be okay," I said, regretting that I had mentioned anything at all. "Let's ask the angels to help us. They love little children."

Johnny began to say a prayer and then burst into shrieks of delight as he stretched to look out the front window.

"Why are you laughing, Johnny?" I said.

"Don't you see them, Mommy? The angels—they are in front of the car!" he said.

"They are?" I responded.

"Yes, they are playing," he chuckled.

"How many are there, Johnny? What do they look like?" I asked in disbelief.

"There are four of them, Mommy. They are little. They are playing funny games," he giggled.

I could not see anything other than snow and stranded cars. There was no way I could verify if Johnny was seeing angels or just imagining them. But instead of crying, he now laughed. A situation that began as scary ended in delight. And we made it home without incident.

Johnny told Sarah and Andrew about the angels, and though they laughed, they also wondered, *Could it be so?*

Sometime later, we planned an adventure. We hadn't been on a real vacation for years, and we needed the levity it might bring. I had flight miles, a small amount of savings, and vacation days, so it was doable. We flew into Albuquerque, rented a car, and began an almost-two-thousand-mile expedition across northern New Mexico, into Arizona, and back. We traveled through one reservation after another—the Pueblo, Apache, Navajo, Hopi, and Zuni territories—stopping at the adobe ruins of cliff dwellers and the remains of high desert pueblos. We visited the healing site of El Santuario de Chimayo and the miraculous spiral staircase in the Loretto Chapel of Santa Fe and toured the mystical vortexes of

Sedona. We stopped at the Grand Canyon, descended and breath-lessly ascended its trails, and paused at the expansiveness of this natural wonder.

We also white-water rafted down the Rio Grande in Taos, maneuvering amid Class 4 swells and personal apprehensions.

"Come on, Mom, you can do this!" the kids insisted as they climbed into the raft.

"Not a chance—I'll wait here till you get back. I've got my book. I'm set."

"Ma'am," the guide called to me, "your littlest son isn't buckled in. You need to be sure his life jacket is tight across his chest."

"Johnny, come here," I called, but he wasn't paying attention. Finally, I stepped into the raft to buckle him up and the guide threw me a life jacket.

"Put this on, ma'am," he said as he pushed us away from the shoreline. We were moving! The kids had tricked me, and they laughed hysterically. As I soon learned, there is no time for fear on the river, because everything happens too quickly. Between the screams, Johnny's accidental fall into the river, and our laughter, it was an exhilarating trip.

Our seven-day journey took us through mountains and deserts, art galleries and a half dozen or so churches, to a place of much-needed merriment.

Still, I was concerned about Andrew. Ever since his father had beaten him, he had not been himself. It was as though a vital part of him was silenced that day. I searched for programs that might stir his once-robust, adventuresome nature and bring him into his natural strength. When I suggested the possibility of Outward Bound, Andrew was elated. He first attended a short program in the Northeast and then enrolled in a lengthy extreme program in the Colorado Rockies, where all participants spent several days solo. Later, he sent me this letter:

Hey Mom, how are you. I hope this is legible; it's hard to write with a pencil on a map in a rainstorm. Anyway even though you will probably get this letter a while after my return, I still thought it necessary...

Mom, I love you. I really do...One thing this trip has taught me is what is really important and what just isn't. Part of what is important is you. Nothing has ever made it clearer than this trip has...Thank you for being who you are, and for sending me on such an incredible journey. I feel as though I have grown up more in the past two weeks or so than in all my life...

Andrew had experienced his strength, and he had glimpsed my intentions. My tears were only of gratitude.

Sarah's wounds were of a different nature: they were both spiritual and psychological. I wondered about a pilgrimage to a healing site.

"There are several healing sites that people from all over the world visit," I explained. "Would you like to go to one of them?"

"Maybe," she said cautiously. "Where would we go?"

"We could go to Lourdes or Fatima or Assisi or..."

As soon as Sarah heard "Assisi," she perked up.

"Assisi? Where Saint Francis lived?" she asked.

"Yes. Would you like to go there?"

"Could we? I'd love to!" she responded excitedly.

Sarah loved animals and had a menagerie of rabbits, parakeets, and even a prairie dog. She was the first to shriek with delight if she noticed a groundhog on the side of the road or a fat puppy in someone's arms. She knew the legends surrounding Saint Francis—of his talking with the animals, of his taming a ravenous wolf—and because of them, he was her favorite saint.

After we secured passports and arranged our flights, my Jesuit colleagues helped us find inexpensive places to stay in Italy. I bought a map and tour book and packed a suitcase with a few essentials, and we were ready. We departed from JFK and arrived in Rome nine hours later. The following morning, we began our journey by train and bus to Assisi. It was a whirlwind.

The medieval town of Assisi overlooks a peaceful valley of green fields and groves of fig, walnut, and olive trees. Our bus wove through these farmlands as it climbed the hill to the fabled city. In the distance, Assisi appeared golden in the late-afternoon light; the walls enclosing its perimeters glistened white. The bus stopped at the edge of the town, and Sarah and I followed the groups of pilgrims entering through the arched gate.

Cobbled streets led us past small shops and wall shrines to the boardinghouse where we would stay the next several nights. We climbed the worn stone staircase to our room and met our proprietor.

"Father Murphy called me," she said, smiling. "He told me you are *gooood* people."

"He's been very kind to us, and we are most grateful to you for offering to let us stay here," I said.

"You will be happy here," she said in her broken English. "Saint Francis blessed us before he died. Assisi is home for those searching for God." Taking my hand, she said, "This will be your home."

Though we had planned to travel to Perugia and Siena on this brief trip, we fell in love with Assisi and went no farther. Every day we walked for miles, retracing the steps of Saint Francis from the country church of San Damiano, just outside Assisi, to the tiny chapel of Porziuncola, and then up to Saint Francis's cave retreat at the Eremo delle Carceri. Everywhere we went, priests, nuns, and other pilgrims accompanied us.

Each morning, noon, and evening, church bells rang, calling us to prayer. Throughout our visit, groups of devotees spontaneously erupted in song in the town square, a block from our room. A few feet from our doorway, a family restaurant served Italian specialties and the owner played the accordion for his guests. We were surrounded by supplications, celebrations, and mouthwatering aromas.

And while our senses feasted, our hearts rested. The proprietor of our boardinghouse was right: Assisi was *home*.

We visited the Basilica of San Francesco several times during our stay. It beckoned us with its magnificence and with the tomb it cradles. The cathedral has three levels: upper, lower, and crypt. We entered through the lower level, where the Latin inscription above the entrance reads: "Slow down and be joyful, pilgrim. You've reached the hill of paradise." Indeed, we felt we had reached paradise, with stunning thirteenth- and fourteenth-century paintings and frescoes on either side of us, and we slowed down to take in the majesty of it all.

From the lower level, we descended an ancient stone staircase to the candlelit vault where the remains of Saint Francis are housed. Even the noisiest tourists are hushed when they enter this consecrated space. The tomb is but a stone box with iron ties lodged above the altar. Holding the small framed Francis, the lover of nature and mankind, it awaits those who need comfort. Before this simple structure, millions upon millions pray. Like these pilgrims, Sarah and I knelt before the remains, our tears joining those of our sisters and brothers.

"Saint Francis, protect my children." I cried and prayed. "Take them as your own, and help them through life's struggles."

Leaving Assisi was not easy. The picturesque village was a healing balm for our souls. When the time came, though, we reluctantly climbed back onto the bus and watched from our windows as the town disappeared from sight. We said very little to each other as we sat on the train, gazing blankly at the countryside zooming past us. We were absorbed in our adventure of the last days—of frescoes and candles, of cobbled streets and tiny stores, of kind people and friars and nuns. We sat quietly, thinking of Saint Francis and his simple life, and we knew something miraculous had occurred. Softness had settled into our hearts, and peace had replaced our fear.

We arrived at JFK to masses of people rushing to or from their flights, loudspeakers announcing departures and calling to the lost.

As we ventured outside the terminal with our bags in tow, whistles shrilly summoned taxis and vans, and horns parted cars and people. Through this jumble of life we walked, separately pondering the world we had left behind. We had been gone only a week, but it seemed like a lifetime.

Our everyday lives changed quickly after the divorce. I had imagined that it would take a while to sell the house, but it was sold within a few weeks, and I had to rush to find another home for our family. Sarah and I searched neighborhoods and new developments, and then, on a whim, we headed to the country. On a quiet, tree-lined gravel road, about ten miles north of the college, we discovered a magical contemporary cottage tucked into an unclaimed forest. FOR SALE BY OWNER, the sign read, which we translated to mean, *This is your new home.*

The owners graciously invited us to come in, even though we had arrived unannounced that late Sunday morning. Their long-haired wheaten border collie instantly stole Sarah's heart, romping around her as we walked room to room. I was just as taken, but for different reasons. The glass walls facing the forest brought in filtered light, and I could see my children in the backyard and on the deck. I could hear their laughter and the crickets of my childhood. I could feel a fresh beginning.

Navigating mortgages and purchase documents was new for me, but with each step I grew more confident. *I can do this*, I realized, and excitement started to emerge. I rented a truck, and the kids and I loaded it with our belongings. We were immigrants of sorts, hoping for a different form of freedom.

Country living presented lessons for us to learn—how to cut the lawn on the hilly embankments bordering our property with an old riding mower; whom to call when the grass got bright green over the septic tank; what to do when the electricity unexpectedly failed;

how to check the well for water levels; when to summon animal control and when not to…

"Listen, listen!" Sarah cried. "It's a wolf. Don't you hear it? It's circling the house."

She was right—and its howls were unnerving. Sarah, Johnny, and I ran upstairs and looked out from the second-floor deck. The wolf saw us and only howled more. Andrew was unfazed and decided to go outside.

"I don't think it's a wolf," he exclaimed. "I'm going to find out."

"No, Andrew, don't do it!" I quickly yelled, but he was already gone.

From the safety of our indoor perch, we watched as Andrew slowly approached the wolf, speaking softly to it. When he got within ten feet or so, he reached out his hand and the animal came to him.

"I told you it wasn't a wolf," Andrew said, smiling, once he returned indoors. "Wolves are afraid of people; they won't normally attack unless the person is trying to hurt them."

"Well, I think it *is* a wolf, and I'm calling animal control," I said firmly. "We can't have it howling at us all night."

When I reported the incident to the animal control staff, they thanked me and explained that our neighbor had a pet that was part wolf and part dog, and it had wandered off. They apologized for the disturbance and added that the owner would be happy to learn where he could find his *pet*. Andrew let us all know that he had told us so—and I noted that I had much to learn.

There was another time when I had to seek the help of animal control. I had asked Johnny to rake the leaves onto a tarp and carry them into the forest.

"The tarp is in the utility shed," I explained. "Just pull it out, stretch it across the lawn, and rake the leaves into it." This was a simple request, I thought, but Johnny quickly returned to the house.

"There was a snake by the tarp, Mom," he said. "It crawled away, but there might be more."

"I doubt that, Johnny," I replied. "It's simpler to use the tarp, so pull it out of the shed."

"Where there is one snake, there might be more!" he complained.

"Come on, I'll show you," I said impatiently.

We walked together outside to the utility shed. I pulled the tarp out and began to unfold its blue edges. One fold, now another, and...

"Oh my God!" I screamed, jumping back. There were literally dozens upon dozens of snakes swarming inside the tarp.

"I told you so!" Johnny exclaimed, jumping back as well.

We rushed inside the house, and I called my new best friends, animal control. "They are small and dark brown, with yellow stripes," I said breathlessly. "There were probably a hundred of them inside the tarp!"

"You've just described the garter snake," the man said, sounding amused by my alarm. "No need to worry; they won't hurt you. They can have eighty or more snakes in a litter," he added. "Just leave the tarp where it is, and the snakes will slither away."

"Thank you, sir. I really appreciate your explanation," I said sheepishly, imagining that I had given him something to laugh about for some time to come.

The boys quickly settled into our new life in the country. Since Andrew attended the private high school affiliated with the university, the move did not affect him. Johnny, however, had to change schools, because in Connecticut children must attend schools where they reside. He was outgoing, though, and quickly made friends and was recruited for the football team.

As for me, I loved my Connecticut country home—the warmth

of the oak floors, the expanse of forest green beyond the walls of windows, the stone fireplace stretching up to the cathedral ceiling. It was an awe-inspiring retreat of wild blackberries, naughty pileated woodpeckers, and taunting raccoons. When snow fell, even the trees held their breath.

Long, solitary walks through the arched beech trees with Maggie, my diminutive bichon frise, drew me into contemplation. I never felt alone on these walks; rather, I felt accompanied by generations of women, most of whom I did not know, but all of whom shared a story. Together we walked silently, knowingly, under the shelter of a leafy portico. My forested hideaway offered me both the time and the space to begin to dream again.

Sometimes I'd wander farther down the road, to a working farm of pick-your-own fruit and vegetables. "Have a cup of fresh cider," the farmer would say, and then tell me about the apples that season. I'd always return home with a just-out-of-the-oven berry pie and a small carton of cream. There is a simple order and dignity to life in the country.

Surrounded by nature's miracles, I decided to talk with my spiritual director about my concerns with the church. As a divorced woman, I felt like an outcast. Very few people knew about the divorce, but I imagined a large-lettered sign on my forehead that read SINNER, and I felt ashamed.

When I explained my feelings to Father Simon, he was dumbfounded. "Do you really doubt the love of God?" he asked patiently.

"I'm not worried about God," I retorted. "It's the church I have issues with, or it with me."

"Well, we have more work to do," he said, and quickly assigned me two tasks. "When we next meet, I want you to tell me who the church is. And, I'd like you to meditate on John 8:3–11—the story of the adulterous woman."

"But I know who the church is," I asserted.

"If you did, you wouldn't have this struggle," he responded, smiling.

Over the following week, I thought about the two assignments and realized that they were intertwined. The adulterous woman was all of us, for who is without fault? The church was/is humanity, for we are all God's children.

John 8:3-11:

³ *The teachers of the law and the Pharisees brought in a woman caught in adultery. They made her stand before the group* ⁴ *and said to Jesus, "Teacher, this woman was caught in the act of adultery.* ⁵ *In the Law Moses commanded us to stone such women. Now what do you say?"* ⁶ *They were using this question as a trap, in order to have a basis for accusing him.*

But Jesus bent down and started to write on the ground with his finger. ⁷ *When they kept on questioning him, he straightened up and said to them, "Let any one of you who is without sin be the first to throw a stone at her."* ⁸ *Again he stooped down and wrote on the ground.*

⁹ *At this, those who heard began to go away one at a time, the older ones first, until only Jesus was left, with the woman still standing there.* ¹⁰ *Jesus straightened up and asked her, "Woman, where are they? Has no one condemned you?"*

¹¹ *"No one, sir," she said.*

"Then neither do I condemn you," Jesus declared. "Go now and leave your life of sin."

When I met with Father Simon, he asked about my experience of the reading.

"I was very moved by Jesus's tenderness toward the accused woman," I said.

"Tell me more," he urged.

"What impressed me the most was that Jesus looked down and wrote on the ground, when the men brought the woman to him. I think he was distracting the men, making them look at the ground and not the woman, and in doing this he was showing respect to the woman."

"And what did you feel?" my director asked.

"I felt the woman's humiliation and trepidation when the men shoved her in front of Jesus. It broke my heart. And, frankly, I was angry at those men. Why didn't they grab her lover too—why just the woman?"

"Good! Now, tell me, where were you in the scene?"

"I was standing to the side, behind the mob of men. There were other women next to me. We were all watching, waiting to see what Jesus would do."

"What were the men saying?"

"They were saying horrible things. They said she was a whore. They wanted to kill her. They said she should suffer. They shouted at us [the women] and told us to leave. 'You don't belong here,' they said."

"Did you? Did you leave?"

"No, we simply backed up a little bit. But we stayed—we stayed for the woman's sake."

"And when Jesus did not condemn the woman, what did you do?"

"The men had already left, and we rushed to her side, covering her with our cloaks."

"And what did you feel?"

"I strongly felt the presence of God," I explained. "Jesus's love brought me to tears; it still does," I acknowledged, while wiping my eyes. "I felt profound acceptance and love."

"Now, who is the church?"

"I am the church; we are all the church, the body of Christ," I answered.

"And what have you decided regarding this church?"

"I am going to make my peace."

The retreat process had led me to a sisterhood of biblical women who I had not known existed. Many of the assigned readings did not mention women, but when I meditated on the stories, the women manifested. Some were standing silently at the periphery, watching the drama unfold, just as in the story of the adulterous woman; others were preparing and serving the meals or were busy with another life concern. So graphic were my scriptural encounters that I felt as though I had time-traveled. Because of this sense of immediacy, conversation flowed between the characters and me. I felt as though I had known them all my life. Metaphorically I was living in two worlds, the ancient past and the present, and the former was helping the latter. This emboldened me to take the steps I needed to take to bring closure to the divorce.

I decided to apply for an annulment, and less than two months after the divorce, I submitted my papers. Ultimately, I hoped for the church's validation and blessing. Unlike most who apply for an annulment, I was not in another relationship, nor had I any plans for remarriage. My intentions were more metaphysical, more heart-driven.

The annulment process is much misunderstood by those who have not gone through it. Very thorough and fact-based, the process requires the applicant to write an account of her life, beginning with childhood, moving through her courtship and engagement with her former spouse, continuing through the wedding and honeymoon, and culminating in the marriage itself—from its beginning weeks until the marriage is legally terminated. The former spouse has the opportunity to refute any or all information and to supply his own testimony.

The first step of the annulment process involves an initial review by the tribunal, at which time it is decided whether or not there is sufficient merit to proceed. If the response is affirmative, as mine was, witnesses (family, friends, and professionals, such as psychologists and social workers) are contacted and invited to supply necessary information about the person and the marriage itself. Eventually, a member or members of the tribunal meet directly with the applicant. Eight months after my initial application, I was called to a meeting.

My judge was an older priest. For the first few minutes, he explained the process, and, once confident of my understanding, he turned his attention to the details of the marriage.

"You don't mind my tape-recording our session, do you?" the judge asked self-consciously. "It helps me remember when I go through all the information."

"That would be fine," I responded, not knowing what else to say.

I scanned the office as he grappled with the tape recorder. Against the dark paneled walls hung his degrees in social work, canon law, and theology. Below these recognitions rested the remains of broken promises and shattered dreams: papers stacked high, without seeming order.

"My apologies," he said. "I'm no good with technology. Shall we begin now?"

"Sure, I'm ready," I said.

He was a humble man, and his deferential approach calmed my apprehension. As I responded to his questions, I saw that he had heard many stories just like mine. His tenderness bared a heart that had cried for and with his clients.

He questioned me very thoroughly. Even though the meeting was draining and at times painful, I was at peace and I knew I had been heard. The judge never criticized what I said, never corrected me, and never diminished my experience. He simply listened respectfully, asking for more details as considered necessary. Throughout the session, I felt celestial presence. We were not alone, and I knew he, too, was aware of that fact.

I left the meeting with a strong sense of blessing, having known palpable love. I had made my peace—irrespective of the outcome of the deliberation.

About a year later, I received formal notification that my marriage was annulled. The letter explained that a psychiatrist had reviewed the case carefully and submitted a written report to the Diocesan

Tribunal. After studying his report, the Diocesan Tribunal ruled. Finally, after going through all the documentation, the Metropolitan Tribunal of the Archdiocese officially declared the marriage null and void. The church had recognized the truth of my experience.

When a person goes through a divorce, there is no healing and very little pastoral care. The civil authorities simply want the matter settled; they are not interested in the details of the marriage, except as are helpful for arguing the case. In many ways, the person seeking a divorce is but a pawn in an elaborate legal chess game: you go where you are told to go and do what you are told to do. The setting is contentious and threatening.

In contrast, the annulment process is humanizing. The tribunal is not focused on blaming or winning; it is interested in understanding the destructive nature of the relationship in order to help repair the lives of the former partners. Through careful examination of volumes of data, the tribunal decides if one or both of the partners were even capable of a mature relationship when they married. Continuation of a marriage is not seen as an indication of validity; rather, mutual respect, care, and the selflessness of the individuals attest to the strength of the union. By meticulously looking at the personality profiles at the time of the initial contract and following the individuals through the months and years of the marriage, the tribunal is able to judge the sources of pathology and then make a decision as to validity or invalidity. This careful assessment exposes the personality flaws and weaknesses that militate against a true marriage of mind, body, and soul and thus helps the estranged couple make peace with their separate journeys.

My former spouse and I were partners in a lengthy legal marriage. The annulment did not change that fact; rather, it simply declared that in the eyes of the church, we were not capable of a true marriage of mind, body, and soul. Our legal contract bound us to laws prescribed by the state; our religious contract included promises to love and cherish each other. Ideally, these two contracts should be one and the same; in our case, only one was valid.

The annulment process was a journey of forgiveness. The months of deliberation, accompanied by the guidance I received during the retreat, helped me begin to let go of the sorrows within the marriage. Bishop Desmond Tutu once stated, "Forgiveness does not mean condoning what has been done. It means taking what happened seriously and not minimizing it; drawing out the sting in the memory that threatens our entire existence." My spiritual director would not allow me to minimize or spiritualize the abuse, and because of his determined stance, I learned to draw out the sting. This was both a doggedly rational process and a spiritual one. I was not just forgiving my former spouse for what had occurred in our marriage; I was pardoning dreams, and I was absolving myself.

Forgiving Ron involved concrete situations—it was straightforward, measurable. As I let go of the past, the dynamics between him and me shifted. He moved on with his life, and I moved on with mine. Interestingly, what remains in my heart toward him is akin to feelings of awkwardness. When I look back over the years, it is like seeing characters in a play. I recognize the protagonist but don't know the performer. When I see or hear about him, it feels as though I am looking at or hearing about a stranger, someone I do not know. And yet this stranger and I parented four beautiful children.

Pardoning my dreams was a different process altogether. I liken it to sitting in my favorite easy chair and slowly turning the frayed pages of my journals that stretch back through time. I pay homage to the dreams that were birthed in my childhood, to the hopes that flowered in my adolescence, and I recognize the betrayals that clouded visions and innocent intentions. I read through the pages and allow my clenched tears to run free. And then, when I hear my heart sigh, *It is finished*, I close the volumes for the last time. I take them outside, and beneath the oak tree that stands tall beside my house, I give them a different home. They were good dreams, I acknowledge—but they were only dreams.

Forgiving myself was more complex than releasing the landscapes of the past. There was no beginning and end; *I* was the constant, not time. Standing figuratively before the mirror of life, I stared at my young self and my old self, each with her separate experiences of joy and sorrow, and each with her separate triumphs and failures. When I looked at the different faces of me, I thought, *If I only had done this or that differently.*

In the movie *The Mission*, there is a haunting image of Robert De Niro climbing up a mountainside, dragging a massive bag filled with armor, guns, stones, and other heavy things. Time and time again, he stumbles and falls back down the slope, only to pick up his bag once more to drag it behind him as he tries to reach the summit. The bag is his self-imposed penance for his wrongdoings. He is so attached to atonement that he is willing to sacrifice his life in the process. He simply cannot forgive himself for his past.

Much like De Niro's character, I felt like a failure and believed I needed to earn absolution. "What if" questions—*What if I lose my job? What if I can't support my family? What if I am shunned?*— harassed me and gave me little peace. And so I stared at the mirror with the time-lapse images, not sure how to make amends. There is no greater judge than our own inner critic. It tortures us as no one else can.

In her book, *Dying to Be Me*, Anita Moorjani shares her realizations while recovering from a near-death experience. Of her encounter, she writes:

> *There was nobody punishing me. I finally understood that it was me I hadn't forgiven, not other people. I was the one who was judging me, whom I'd forsaken, and whom I didn't love enough. It had nothing to do with anyone else...I saw that I'd never loved myself, valued myself, or seen the beauty of my own soul.*

Like Anita, I had not "seen the beauty of my own soul." I had grown so attached to my weighty bag of shortcomings, disappointments, failures, and mistakes that I had lost who I was. Through my lengthy annulment process and accompanying retreat, I realized that forgiveness is both letting go of our heartaches and dreams and coming home to ourselves. It is a process of recovering joy—through rediscovering who we are.

Unfinished Business

At my Connecticut refuge, I awoke to hawks soaring past my curtainless windows and went to sleep with the moon and stars shimmering through the swaying trees. I was pampered by the sounds of the nearby creek and entertained by four-legged creatures. Cradled in this natural beauty, my heart began to sing.

After four years of this magical interlude, though, an opportunity arose at a college in California that was difficult to ignore. The new position was similar in many ways to my current role, but it also offered new responsibilities that enticed me. I was torn about what to do. On the one hand, my extended family lived in California, and a move would bring me closer to those I loved—and farther away from memories that needed to fade. On the other hand, I treasured my fairy-tale home and its proximity to New York City, where both Matt and Sarah now lived. Not knowing what to do, I finally decided to apply for the position and wait.

Months passed, and I forgot about my application. When the phone call finally came, I was ill-prepared.

"Hello, Gwen. I'm calling from Pacific Groves College to invite you for an interview," the president of the college said.

"Pacific Groves College?" I responded, trying to place the name.

"Yes, you applied for the position advertised in the *Chronicle of Higher Education* four months ago."

"Yes, yes…my apologies. I am working on another matter right now and wasn't expecting your call."

"Could you come for an interview in two weeks?" he asked.

"I believe so," I said, searching for my calendar.

"Wonderful. I'll have my secretary work out the details with you. Safe journey!"

"Thank you. I look forward to meeting you," I replied. As I hung up the phone, I sat thinking, *What just happened?*

After work that day, I researched the college and the area, as I knew little about either. Later, I mentioned the possibility to Andrew and Johnny. They associated California with relatives, the desert, and beaches. Both were noncommittal but understood why I might be interested. Andrew was enrolled in classes at the university where I worked, where tuition was waived for the children of employees. He would need to transfer elsewhere if I accepted the job, because the tuition costs were beyond our means. Johnny was a senior in high school and didn't say much one way or the other, though he mentioned that he could live with his friends to finish the year. At that point in time, the new role was simply a distant possibility anyway; therefore, without anything to lose, I flew out and met with my prospective colleagues.

Several weeks after the interview, I was offered the position, and though I felt honored to have been selected, I was uncertain about what to do. I struggled with nagging questions: *Will I be able to support the kids? Will I be successful in my job? Will Andrew and Johnny be okay in their new schools?* The college wanted an answer that day, but I could not give them one. Finally they said I had a week to decide.

Over the weekend, while the boys were out with their friends, I contended with my fear. Sitting on the deck with my eyes closed, listening to the breeze whispering through the leaves, I imagined myself walking through the woods to a beautiful pasture of wildflowers and butterflies, across a meandering clear river with gentle rapids and swells, and up a steep rocky mountain of boulders and pine trees. I traveled with my fears, but before I reached the pinnacle, they deserted me.

In the silence of vast imaginary mountain ranges and open blue skies, I felt a profound sense of divine presence, and in that moment, I knew what I would do. It was time to leave the past, with its tumultuous highs and lows, and begin afresh, where the present was what mattered most.

When I shared my decision with a friend, she read me Edgar Lee Masters's poem "George Gray":

> *I have studied many times*
> *The marble which was chiseled for me—*
> *A boat with a furled sail at rest in a harbor.*
> *In truth it pictures not my destination*
> *But my life.*
> *For love was offered me and I shrank from its disillusionment;*
> *Sorrow knocked at my door, but I was afraid;*
> *Ambition called to me, but I dreaded the chances.*
> *Yet all the while I hungered for meaning in my life.*
> *And now I know that we must lift the sail*
> *And catch the winds of destiny*
> *Wherever they drive the boat.*
> *To put meaning in one's life may end in madness,*
> *But life without meaning is the torture*
> *Of restlessness and vague desire—*
> *It is a boat longing for the sea and yet afraid.*

I flew back to California the next weekend to look for a home, and within hours of my return flight to Connecticut, I signed papers to secure my new abode. The same week, my beloved country retreat sold to newlyweds longing for a place to raise a family. Everything happened rapidly. Much like with the white-water-rafting trip, we had no time to be afraid. We had less than a month to pack our possessions and either give away a household of belongings or leave them to the new owners.

Over Christmas vacation, we said our good-byes, loaded a moving van, and headed to the West Coast. Andrew and Johnny followed me in their red hatchback Honda Civic. I drove with Maggie, who imagined herself to be copilot, sitting on top of the suitcases and boxes shoved tightly together in the back of my Outback. The boys and I kept in touch with each other through the two-way radios that I had purchased at a local camping store. "Mom, we're getting hungry," they'd let me know with regularity. Who knew that travel prompts starvation in adolescent boys?

AAA advised us to take the southern route. "It will be a safer drive," the representative explained, "because it will be warmer than the northern route through Salt Lake City." Travel was easy until we entered West Virginia, where snow began to fall. Somewhere in the Appalachian Mountains, we hit an unprecedented arctic front that iced the roads and our resolve. "One of the worst this century," people said. We watched eighteen-wheeler trucks burn to the ground in front of us after spinning out of control on the ice. Then pickups slammed into the back of these road monsters. We pulled off the freeway and waited until a lane opened up; then, passing the charred remains of the semi trucks, we continued driving until we found a fast-food restaurant. This was a journey for which we had not prepared.

Even with the weather difficulties, we arrived at our new home in California several days before the moving van and just two days before Christmas. With our sleeping bags and stray pillows, we set up camp in the empty living room and began exploring the area. We could not go far, because the moving van was due to arrive at any time. Nevertheless, on Christmas Day we decided to drive to the nearby ski slopes. "This will be our Christmas," I told the boys. "We'll rent equipment and enjoy a day in the snow." Both Andrew and Johnny were avid snowboarders, and they were elated.

There were no lines for the lifts on this clear winter morning, just my sons and a few skiers wearing hijabs. I brought a good book to read and between the pages would look up to see them creating their own trails in the fresh snow. While most folks were home, opening gifts, sitting around their warm fireplaces, or preparing a scrumptious meal for their loved ones, we enjoyed the refreshment of Heavenly Mountain by Lake Tahoe.

Moving from one college to another has a comfortable familiarity. There is universality to the quest for knowledge, irrespective of the physical environment. College communities bear the aspirations of people of all backgrounds and shoulder the laudable responsibility of providing the means for students to reach their goals. At its best, the college community is an extraordinary center of transformation.

My responsibilities at Pacific Groves covered the student-support departments: admissions, counseling, financial aid, health services, matriculation, and more. I was the recourse for students (and their parents) if perceived rights or benefits were not met. Because of the proximity of the college to military bases, one of my areas of responsibility became the waves of veterans who were enrolling in classes with hopes of getting the education their military recruiters had promised them.

This special population of young men and women arrived with the visible and invisible scars of combat. Several had Purple Hearts and military recognitions. Many were Wounded Warriors. They had lived on alert and in fear for lengthy periods of time, and now they were in an academic setting where they had very different demands and expectations.

Veterans returning from combat need time to transition to civilian life. To move from a battlefield to a classroom, to shift from taking commands to deciding one's own course of action, is no simple task. Many of these students have lost friends in war, and most have come close to death themselves. Soldiers do not leave the battlefield just because they have signed discharge papers. The battlefield travels with them.

When veterans enroll in a college, they enter with far more than school supplies; they arrive with their backpacks of war experiences, their physical and mental disabilities, and their lost youth. They may have known active duty for only a year or so, but during this period, their world was turned upside down as they endured a lifetime of extremes. Transitioning to civilian life for the newly returned veteran is a challenge that colleges are ill prepared to assist in helping them surmount.

College communities are diverse, and because of the multiplicity of interests and ethnicities therein, clashes of perspective happen. Students are encouraged to speak up, to voice their points of view, and to question the status quo. For student veterans, however, this boldness can be confusing, because the issues themselves can seem insignificant. They are not concerned about the quality of paper napkins in the cafeteria; they are not interested in whether the coffee cart carries pumpkin spice or peppermint mocha. The concerns of the returning veterans are concrete and pressing. They struggle with post-traumatic stress disorder; they struggle with maneuvering within an educational system that can seem at odds with their military training; they struggle with Veterans Affairs and the funding they have been promised but have not received. They struggle with *survival* issues, which they wrongly assumed they were leaving behind when they finished their tour of duty.

Ideally, these young men and women need to be mentored by seasoned veterans who have successfully integrated into civilian life. These older veterans can help guide the newer ones through the minefields of the past, through the in-between world they now occupy, and to their soon-to-be home in the United States. For this process to occur, a gathering site is vital. Because no such space was initially available at the college, I offered to share my administrative area until a permanent solution could be created. That decision resulted in an unexpected realization.

The veterans quickly formed a community in their adopted space. Leaders emerged who actively worked on critical issues, including morale, finances, and grades. The veterans monitored and pushed one another to succeed. They tutored those who needed assistance and competed for grades. When one of their colleagues was struggling, they collectively pitched in and helped. They became a family.

One day I walked out of my office and toward the veterans' area, and in a flash of a second, I noticed something that sent shock waves through me. A new veteran sat at a ninety-degree angle to me; his side faced the hallway down which I was walking. As I neared the area, I observed the veteran's muscles tense, I noticed how he quickly turned to see who was approaching, and I saw the fear in his eyes. In that fleeting second, I saw myself.

I have never dealt with the severe circumstances that our military endures, but I have known a prolonged threat of a different nature. Through the veterans, I finally understood the anxiety I felt when I heard a door open or close, why I tensed when I heard footsteps that I was not expecting, why I couldn't sit with my back to a window. I understood, by seeing the extremes of post-traumatic stress disorder in the vets, why I had felt anxious for decades when I heard certain sounds or when I was in certain settings. I understood why I was always vigilant.

A marine tried to explain his reality in an English paper, which he then gave me permission to share. He wrote:

I am a grown man, so why am I scared of the dark?

I am scared of the dark! I have to have some form of light or noise at night, or I will be absolutely paranoid and unable to fall asleep. If I wake up in the middle of the night (which happens every night) to go to the restroom, I first look out my bedroom door and then I either walk fast or run to the restroom. I always have the feeling that someone is watching me in the dark, waiting for me to put my guard down so that they can attack. Sometimes as I stare into the darkness in the hallway, I think I see someone there, again, just waiting. It makes my heart drop into my stomach, and I get really nervous.

My mind knows that this is not true, that no one is waiting for me. I know that it is crazy to be afraid of the dark, but my body feels and tells me something totally different. My body tells me to feel scared, nervous, paranoid, ready, alert, on edge, and willing to protect myself if need be. I feel all of these feelings at the same time.

Can you imagine living your life like this for seven months straight, day after day, and tell me you wouldn't be worried? I had to constantly watch my back, my surroundings, and listen to every little thing. I knew in my mind that at the barracks I had backup, but I was still paranoid because they had no doors. I often thought that I was going to be killed in my sleep.

I still feel like I have to be on alert 24-7. I say to myself, No one here poses a threat to you. But it still feels that way. People tell me I'm crazy and that I shouldn't be afraid of the dark, or that's the past and [I should] get over it, but that is part of the reason why I wrote this. For those people, because they don't understand and will never understand what this feels like, then...and now...

Though I did not know it at the time, my passion to assist the veteran population on campus was linked to my personal journey and to that of my children. Violence is violence, and whether its origin is noble (as in the case of the veterans) or ignoble (as had been my family's experience), the toll of violence is profound. I have lived with post-traumatic stress disorder for more than forty years, and I don't know if it ever truly leaves. I do know, however, that extreme anxiety can dissipate with time—if one is in a safe and supportive environment. I was determined to create such an environment for the veterans returning from war. They deserved a safe place in which to regroup and begin their healing.

Working with the veteran community on campus was a highlight of my career. Their struggles were heartbreaking, but their commitment was inspirational. When I dealt with a situation that evoked the clamors of familiar terrors, it was the veterans who unknowingly guided me with their courage and steadfastness. The circumstances of the threat were different from what I had known earlier in my life, but the core challenge was the same.

Because of my role, it was up to me to resolve complaints regarding work conditions and harassment. On one occasion, a young employee alleged an illegal situation involving drugs in the office where she worked. She was frightened to speak because she was afraid of retaliation. I worked with human resources to settle the case, but the situation escalated. Key office staff discovered who had spoken, and though the employee had whistle-blower protection, that did not stop the scapegoating that ensued. One of her outspoken colleagues stated firmly, "You think this is about truth. It's not about truth. It's about winning!"

"So, facts are irrelevant?" I retorted.

"As I said, it's about winning, and we will win!" he stated defiantly. "You need my support. You can't make it without me!" he ranted.

As he continued his tirade, I suffered the same gut-wrenching fear symptoms of years before and then realized this was my unfinished business. This time I was figuratively pushed against a wall; instead of having a fork pressed into my cheek, I saw my livelihood dangled precariously in front of me. In that moment, I made the decision to confront the vestiges of my fear head-on.

"It's your choice to do whatever you are going to do," I responded. "As for me, I will proceed in truth; I will not bow to intimidation."

Through the span of this lengthy case, I learned a lot. I realized how incivility can be embedded and protected in institutions when politics takes priority over truth, when people place their prospects

of advancement ahead of doing what is right. Fear is a notable moti-
vator, and there are those who are uncanny in their ability to use it
for their benefit. But, I've also come to see that such people do not
act alone; it takes at least two—one who does the pushing, one who
receives it. If we are capable of choice at the time of intimidation,
then we have more power than we might imagine.

While I was in the throes of the college drama, my daughter
called, inviting me to lunch. She had just returned from an eight-
day residential workshop at the Hoffman Institute in the Napa
Valley, and she wanted to share her experience. We met at a little
restaurant close to the college. As soon as I saw her, I was struck by
her radiance.

"You look wonderful, Sarah," I said as we embraced.

"Mom, you would love the program. It's just your kind of thing,"
she said, smiling. "You should sign up for the spring program!"

"Eight days? Seems like a long time. I don't know if I can take off
that much time," I replied.

"It runs through two weekends, so you will miss only five days
of work," she insisted.

"Okay, I'll consider it. Where can I find more information?" I
asked.

"Oh, I hoped you would ask! I brought it with me," she said with
a playful smile.

The image of my daughter's smile kept teasing me with hope.
The conflict with the irate employee was exhausting, and I longed
for relief. Finally, I read through the literature and learned that the
focus of the program is personal discovery and development. I
talked with the Hoffman staff, who answered some of my questions,
and then decided to enroll in the spring program. Within days I
received a lengthy pre-Hoffman questionnaire that students are
required to fill out. It took at least a day to respond thoughtfully to
its copious questions about my personal and family history, and to
identify behavior patterns that my parents and I shared.

I flew into Sacramento and drove from there to St. Helena in the heart of wine country, where White Sulphur Springs, the California home of the Hoffman Institute, is located. It was a hot-springs resort in decades long past. Tucked into the hills, aging wooden structures abut a thick redwood grove crisscrossed by paths and a babbling creek.

I parked my car in the gravel lot next to the registration building and breathed the crisp spring air deeply. *This* is *my kind of place*, I thought. The harried world at the college, of human privations and political gyrations, gave me little reprieve; here, silence echoed through the narrow canyon. I never would have imagined that my tranquil sanctuary would soon become a deafening sweatshop.

Sarah had told me little about the actual mechanics of her time at the Hoffman Institute, even though she was very encouraging. Since I was a bit of a retreat-workshop enthusiast, I was ready for one more that might be the elixir my soul desired.

On the first morning, twenty-four participants convened with five or so facilitators. We knew each other by first name only. It was curious being among a group whose members had no other identity. We were history-less for this week, without job titles, degrees, successes, or failures; all of this was restricted information.

The first order of business was to meet with my assigned teacher—the person who would accompany me through the next eight days. He was a little older than I was, kindly and very understanding. He had been a minister and a counselor before joining the staff at the institute. I was elated when I met him; I sensed that he would understand me, and thus I felt safe.

My teacher handed me a notebook and explained that I would be doing a lot of writing both during and after the exercises. Then he reviewed my lengthy application, asked some clarifying questions, and explained a few aspects of the program. I understood from him that the course would focus on the beliefs and patterns of behavior that all of us incorporate from our parents, and they from their parents.

"We'll meet every day to review your experience, but if something comes up, I'm always available to talk. Do you have any questions?" he asked.

"Actually, I do. Someone mentioned that we will be hitting a pillow with a plastic baseball bat. Is that true?" I asked, quite aware that my question seemed childish, if not foolish.

"Yes, that is true. It's part of the curriculum," he explained haltingly.

"Well, I won't do that," I stated promptly.

"You will, Gwen. Everyone does it," he answered with a smile.

"Well, maybe *everyone* does it, but not me," I said firmly.

"When they start hitting the pillow, you will find it easy to do," he added patiently. "No one will even notice you."

"Truly, I don't think I'll be joining in this exercise," I responded defiantly. I knew I would prove him wrong.

Within a day, we were given an assignment that included bashing a pillow. As I look back on this, I can't help but chuckle. I'm an introvert by nature, and I recoil at public displays, but I was in a room with twenty-three others who started pounding their pillows with gusto. The once-quiet space was now filled with rhythmic beating, bashing, thumping sounds. People were vocalizing their frustrations: "I hate you, I hate you!" some shouted, hitting harder. Others cursed at the pillow: "Fuck you!" they'd scream, red-faced. Feeling awkward about my defiance, I picked up my bat and started to hit the pillow—timidly at first, then harder, until finally I joined my colleagues in pounding it with all my strength. A lot of emotions were surfacing, and that scared me. I felt rage, indignation, resentment, shame, hate; I felt emotions that I had hidden even from myself. Motivated by history and yearning, I struck the pillow as hard as I could.

That night I could not sleep; I was tormented by remnants, ghosts from the past. I knew I was not the only one facing skeletons, because throughout the night I could hear colleagues still bashing their pillows in the meeting room. Cuddled under the blankets, I waited for daylight. When the morning arrived, we gathered for deeper personal work, which again required us to hit the pillow. I didn't wait this time—I decided to deal with my demons.

The exercises were emotionally demanding because they tapped into primal fears and not-so-conscious negative behavioral patterns. Unfinished business showed up as part of a continuum that stretched deep into childhood. Throughout the week, attendees were both participants and spectators as they traced their current behavioral approaches to their origins. The assignments addressed all aspects of self—emotional, intellectual, physical, and spiritual. Just when the work (and it *is* work) became overwhelming, the exercises shifted and became less grueling. Then, midway through the process, play was introduced through music, dance, and theatrics.

Of all the features of the program, the one that was the most difficult but also the most powerful for me was the play exercise. I found it very hard to be a child, to be carefree. In the end, I felt sick and asked to return to my room, but the teachers would not let me. And so I sat off to the side and watched.

I envied those who spontaneously danced about the room to Michael Jackson and Cyndi Lauper, those who mischievously pretended to be Disney characters with long noses or big ears, those who excitedly blew up balloons and draped paper streamers across the windows for an afternoon party. I both yearned for and feared their spirited laughter, their emergent comedic freedom.

As the solitary bystander in a crowded room of frolicking adult children, I traveled back in time—to when I was just a toddler taking care of my baby sister, imagining I was so big; to when my dad returned home from the hospital with his stub of an arm and I attempted to make him smile; to when Mom lost one of her babies and nearly her own life and I became the one to care for the family. I traveled from childhood to adulthood—to when I fell in love with and then said my good-byes to Bruce and later to Ron, to the birth of each of my children, and to my various jobs. Sitting on the sidelines of the revelry, I walked through my snapshots of weighted memories. Once again I thought about the baby picture of the toddler me sitting in front of a Christmas tree with a full-faced smile, and again I recalled my therapist's question "What makes you happy?" As I watched my colleagues' obvious joy, I realized how tightly I was holding on inside—but to what?

My tears swelled as buried emotions fought for expression. I realized that I did not know how to be a child, because the child me was hiding—under layers of fear, judgment, and expectations. And instantaneously I understood that the child me awaited discovery and embrace. She alone could teach me how to play. But how could I reach her?

This pivotal moment changed my experience of the Hoffman workshop. I glimpsed a direction to the workshop exercises; I understood why we labored at identifying learned patterns of behavior, and the undeniable relationship between times past and times present.

Over the days that followed, my view of my previous choices and decisions shifted. Instead of blaming myself or others for perceived mistakes or injustices, I realized that I had done the best I could at the time, and that most likely those involved in my past struggles had done so as well. With this realization came empathy for my younger self. I began to forgive from a place of deep acceptance. This vital retracing, reinterpreting, and retelling of my story led me through the tangled jungles of my past sorrows to the innocent inner child patiently awaiting me.

We are always a work in progress, but by listening and responding to the voices lodged defiantly within our hearts, we emerge in the present with greater freedom to be who we are. When my patterns began to soften and sometimes dissolve through the different Hoffman exercises, compassion emerged. Slowly I was brought to a place of reverential silence, a sacred place in which I could look upon my younger self with tenderness and gratitude.

On the final night of the program, we had a candlelit integration ceremony. Through a lengthy visualization, participants faced imaginary hurdles of life and were helped to identify with their inherent strength. When the meditation concluded, the lights came back on and, standing behind me, waiting to greet me, was my beautiful daughter. She had driven five hundred miles that day just to embrace me.

"Congratulations," Sarah said with open arms. "I love you so much, and I'm so proud of you."

"I love you more than you'll ever know," I cried. "Thank you for coming; I had no idea you'd be here."

"I have a little something for you," she said. "It's not much, but when I saw this print, I thought of you. It's called *A Prayer to Our Lady of Everything*, by Shiloh Sophia McCloud."

our lady of everything
precious mother
hail, ma abundant
so full of grace
blessed art thou
among all mothers and daughters
we who know you
beyond titles and concepts
blessed is the life-giving fruit
of your tree of life womb
wholey mary-ma
mother of god
praise you for praying
for us now and in
every hour of need
you love us
with everything you are
holding us
in your eternal embrace

beloved cosmic matrix from
which we came
wrap us as a babe
in your blue robe of stars
rock us on your seat of wisdom
sing us your songs
of rose petals and justice
dance christ's love into our bones
keep us, precious mother
cradled in your milky way
our lady of faith
may we walk the path of truth
that sets us free
teach us
how to share your love
with our earthly family
blessed be our
mother of everyone
our lady of everything

When I drove away from the White Sulphur Springs campus the next morning, I said good-bye to a family of teachers who gave up their nights along with us, to my classmates who braved their past and their lingering fears, and to the ancient redwoods that comforted me as surely as they must have consoled others through the years. I realized as I drove away that I was tired, very tired, of running from fear, of living on edge for some unknown threat. I was ready to let it all go—to soar free.

I drove through the Napa Valley to Interstate 80, unfazed by the beckoning of one winery after another—the Franciscan Winery, Robert Mondavi, Domaine Chandon, and more. When people impatiently honked or struggled to pass one another, I realized that I was not in a hurry. My type-A personality, always ready to take on the next task, was content—to wait patiently at the stoplights, to allow others to cut in front of me, to drive in the slow lane *slowly*. It just did not matter. At one point, I reactivated my cell phone, noticed some seventeen messages, and turned it back off. I was not interested in the latest campus calamity. I wanted time, even just travel time, to let my soul absorb the developments of the last eight days. I wanted to lounge in the vast openness I felt deep within. And as I drove, I thought about my pillow-pounding colleagues and my remarkable daughter. The eight days had been far more meaningful than I had even anticipated.

My flight out of Sacramento after the Hoffman workshop was delayed by two hours because of a mechanical problem. Passengers paced back and forth, repeatedly questioning the ticket agents and otherwise furiously typing on their laptops. This was more than an inconvenience, it seemed, but for me it was actually a relief.

Wanting to hide in a quiet corner with my realizations of the prior eight days, I stalked the surrounding gates until I found an unclaimed space. I felt so tired. *Have I ever been this exhausted before?* I wondered. Not even my manic aerobics classes had evoked such fatigue. I pulled out my journal from my carry-on bag and flipped through its pages in hopes of finding a clue. And there it was—a scribbled note from our last group meeting: *learning how to harmonize my inner and outer realities*, I had written.

Fear had been so much a part of my life that I anticipated it. If I was feeling joyful, I searched for my fear. *Surely it is here*, I would think. *I know it will appear soon.* And once it surfaced, I would always feel a peculiar sense of comfort because I did not have to worry about it anymore. Now, however, fear was nowhere to be found; I simply felt exhaustion. Could it be that I was feeling the effect of vacant dread? Was letting go of fear really that significant?

I thought back to one of my first attempts to meditate: I sat silently on the floor with a pillow under my backside, twisting my body into a vaguely Zen-like pose. Struggling to clear my mind of random thoughts, I squirmed with my uncooperative long legs and took several deep breaths. After a few minutes of awkward distraction, inexplicably, I observed myself from the vantage point of the ceiling near the doorway of the room. I stared down at my person, quite perplexed.

She looks so frightened, my elevated me thought. *Look how tight she holds her body. What is she so worried about?* The ceiling me was quite bemused by the floor me. And in this rare moment, I perceived myself both as free of all worries and as trapped. I had never experienced anything like this before (nor have I since then), so I attributed the bilocation to a fluke of meditation. But now, as I sat in my space near a Southwest Airlines gate, I thought back to this unusual occurrence and I wondered, *Which is the true me—the self who is boundless, light, and happy, or the self who is tied up inside? Is this what the teachers were talking about when they spoke of making the two realities "congruent"?*

Finally the ticket agent announced that it was time to board, and passengers rushed to the gate. I was in no hurry, and waited until the stampede had passed before I embarked. My seat was next to a kindly woman who was much too large for her space.

"I'm so sorry," she said as soon as I sat down. "I'll try to be small," she added, pulling her arms across her chest.

"I have all the space I need, so don't worry about me," I replied, thinking that she had articulated what I had been trying to do all my life—make myself small. I was content sitting snugly and silently next to her, thinking about the past week and the road ahead.

Returning to work was a test of no small measure. I was greeted with a stack of documents needing signatures, a lineup of meetings for which I was chair, and appointments of employees and students seeking assistance. As I listened, advised, and deliberated, I was aware that I wasn't caught in my usual angst and I was speaking freely. The Hoffman exercises had wiped my soul of its fear, and with that, I was seeing things more clearly—and what I saw gave me pause.

I had always been able to walk into a room and sense the social dynamics. I would know intuitively who was upset or disinterested or scheming, and if I was leading the discussion or assisting someone else in his or her effort, I would anticipate the needs of the group through the unspoken chorale of emotions. Sitting by a person, I'd sometimes feel his or her inner struggles or their joys. This innate ability had assisted me through the years and sometimes overwhelmed me.

Now I recognized an added dimension to what I instinctively knew: fear was at the heart of each sad story or unfolding drama. While one person might be afraid of losing a job, another was anxious about real or imaginary travails, and still others hid their fear under the veil of one conspiracy theory after another. The bullies among them were frightened of loss of power and exposure; the timid feared being and expected to be ignored and sacrificed.

As I listened, I wondered what would happen if we were able to collectively pause and then act from a position of truth. What if we could trust that what was said was meant and we did not have to sort through the weeds of deception to find the threads of candor? If we could stand on common ground, wouldn't there be greater balance, wholesomeness? And wouldn't such a stance affect the entire college? For as much as we reel against institutions, be they brick and mortar or political, aren't they simply a reflection of the collective *we*? My eight-day retreat helped me realize that I could not accept controlling or intimidating behavior—no matter who might engage in such conduct.

Within a week of returning to campus, I walked out the upstairs back door of my office building and noticed a student sitting on the high stone staircase, inching closer to the edge. As I slowly approached him, I spoke calmly and quietly. When I reached his side, I asked him why he was sitting there.

"I want to hurt myself," he said with a vacant smile as he looked far below to the patio. "I wonder what it would feel like. Would there be a lot of pain?"

"I think there would be considerable pain, but maybe much worse than just pain. You could be permanently disabled, or you could die," I said. "Why would you want to hurt yourself?"

"I need to punish myself," he said matter-of-factly. "I'm a disgrace to my family."

"I am sure you are not a disgrace," I said. "I have four children; two of them are around your age. No matter what my kids might do, I would never want them to hurt themselves. Your parents feel the same about you."

The student disagreed and explained that he had gotten a lower grade on a test than he expected. He wanted to punish himself so that he would never make the same mistake again. We talked a bit more and then he agreed to go with me to the health center, where he could get supportive counseling.

On another occasion, a student climbed over a glass guardrail and was standing on a few inches of flooring, staring down into the lobby of the building. Much as I had with the prior student, I approached her calmly, talking about insignificant matters. When I was next to her, I asked her why she was standing there. She turned and looked at me with utter despair. She did not speak. I placed my hand on hers, told her how beautiful she was, and stated that I wanted to know her. I explained that she could trust me and that she could not stand on the ledge. Finally I asked her to come with me. Together we walked to the health center and got assistance. She, too, had not done well on a test, and she was afraid that her parents would be very upset with her. The only solution within her grasp, she believed, was to punish herself through physical pain.

These two students perceived themselves as failures, and they acted out what most of us do regularly through our thoughts. We berate ourselves. We refuse to forgive ourselves. We often judge ourselves more harshly than anyone else might. We torture ourselves in this way, rather than accept ourselves for who we are—with our imperfections but also with our splendor. This is our ultimate unfinished business, and it accompanies us throughout life. It tags along like an unwanted stray, begging for our attention. When we face that which we do not want to see or perhaps that which we have buried deep within, we step onto hallowed ground and walk with the angels. As we do so, we discover truths that untie our hearts and free our souls. Our resolution creates the possibility of greater joy.

Joan Tollifson writes in her book *Awake in the Heartland: The Ecstasy of What Is*:

> *Life always gives us exactly the teacher we need at every moment. This includes every mosquito, every misfortune, every red light, every traffic jam, every obnoxious supervisor (or employee), every illness, every loss, every moment of joy or depression, every addiction, every piece of garbage, every breath. Every moment is the Guru.*

Rather than focusing on who is right or who is wrong, Tollifson focuses on our choices in the moment. If life is indeed the teacher, then the question is: *What am I to learn from this experience?* And in that light, our difficulties become opportunities—to rechart our way, to reclaim our spirit—through our choices.

I doubt we are ever completely free of our old business, but I know that when we surrender our armor of self-judgment and embrace our shortcomings, rather than persecute ourselves for them, we move into authenticity. From this position of humbled strength, we are capable of true forgiveness of long-held hurts. We don't excuse the wounding behavior; rather, we see it for what it is and let it go, because we no longer need to hold on to that which does not belong to us. When we take back our power and control, we are free.

It is easy for any of us to *say* we forgive; it is easy for us to *recite* the Lord's Prayer. What *isn't* easy and what requires profound courage and magnanimity, however, is actually letting go of deeply hidden hurts—our suppressed anger over the molestation of our child, dormant bitterness toward an abusive spouse, desire for revenge toward anyone who has threatened or taken the life of someone we love. If we are honest with ourselves, we will admit that true forgiveness for any such atrocity is very difficult. I thought I had pardoned the individuals involved in the sorrows of my life—until I started pounding my pillow at the Hoffman Institute. Only when I allowed myself to really experience the darkness of unforgiveness through that very physical and lengthy exercise did I realize that I had buried my feelings by spiritualizing the situations. We cannot let go of feelings that we do not know exist.

True forgiveness for me has been and is a progression of faltering baby steps through a storm of flying debris. With time, I have learned to walk more freely. I stand alone, but the universe accompanies me.

Angels Among Us

My arrival home from the Hoffman Institute was revelatory in other ways as well. The first time I walked into my empty house, I had the strong sense that I would not be there long. It felt different now, as though it had completed its task. It had nurtured me through work calamities, supported the boys as they transitioned from high school into college, been a launching pad for Sarah as she pursued her career, and befriended me at night when I sat alone. It had been a good home, a safe home—but as I walked through the rooms, I felt as though I was saying good-bye. I knew I would be leaving the house, but I did not know when. Similarly, when I returned to campus and addressed the roller coaster of human needs, I knew I would not be at the college much longer. My heart was elsewhere, even though I wasn't sure where *elsewhere* might be.

Then my sister called.

"Hey, Gwen. One of my friends lost his wife a while ago, and he told me he was ready to be introduced to someone. Are you interested in meeting him?" she asked.

"Hmm, I don't know," I replied, thinking about the caution of the tribunal judge at the annulment hearing. "Take your time; don't make this mistake again," he had warned. "If you meet someone, make sure he is a good person. Ask your friends; ask your family." At the time, I had had no intention of meeting anyone, but I had always known I would eventually know real love; it was part of what I needed to learn from life.

"What kind of person is he?" I finally asked.

"I've known him for years, Gwen. His deceased wife was my best friend. He's a good man," she offered. "I could invite both of you to dinner and—"

"Okay," I interrupted, "but only if the two of us meet where we can get up and leave if we don't feel comfortable. So it can't be at your house. Have him call me, okay?"

At a restaurant midway between our separate homes, my future husband and I met for the first time. We both arrived early for the rendezvous—he in his pickup, I in my car—and accidently intersected at the restaurant door.

"Are you Gwen?" he asked shyly.

"Yes, and you must be Larry," I responded. "How did you know who I was? Did my sister describe me?"

"She did," he smiled, and quickly added, "but she didn't do you justice."

We found a table in a corner of the restaurant, and then this tall, handsome, and quiet-spoken gentleman presented me with a chocolate rose. In all my years of marriage, I had never been given such a thoughtful, kindly gift.

"I know it's not much," he said, "but I didn't know what to bring."

"You didn't need to bring anything, but this is perfect," I replied. "I love chocolate!"

Larry and I talked about the simple things in life, about our families and our interests. We laughed about the joys of grandchildren and touched upon the sorrows we had each known. And then his expression changed and he became more serious.

"I want you to know that I don't play games," he said.

I didn't know what to say, because I wasn't sure if he was referring to Monopoly or Scrabble or speaking about something more existential.

"Which games don't you like?" I finally ventured.

"Oh, I don't mean board games," he chuckled. "I was referring to the games people play with one another. I don't play games with people. What I say, I mean."

"My goodness, you just scored major brownie points! I don't play games either—and what I say, *I* mean." And we both laughed heartily.

When we finally said good-bye, we knew we were actually saying hello. From that time forward, we were a couple, and for each subsequent date, Larry brought me a bag or box of chocolates.

Over the months that followed, we drove back and forth to see each other—to Larry's home in the Inland Empire, southeast of Los Angeles, to mine on the periphery of Orange County, close to the Pacific Ocean. Each home, with its empty rooms, beckoned another beginning.

When Larry and I got together, it was both a prolonged letting go of memorials to dreams, to sorrows, to what could have been but wasn't, and the launch of a new life. We took road trips to places we had not visited—to Hearst Castle, to the Solvang wineries, to wildlife parks and zoos, and to the mountains. Each in our own way, we were rediscovering life.

When I was visiting him one day, we decided to drive up to Idyllwild for lunch. Tucked into the woods of the San Jacinto mountain range, the town is framed by the majestic Tahquitz Peak. Its snow-covered pinnacle stands tall behind quaint boutiques and novelty stores, restaurants and cabins. After finishing our meal, we explored the town and happened upon the Queen of Angels church, barely noticeable through the ponderosa pine and cedar trees.

This little chapel has an old-world charm—knotty pine siding, a simple wooden altar, a small organ in the back, and images of times long past. Without thinking, I found myself counting the pews and imagining how many could be seated there. I realized that I was thinking about a wedding—*my* wedding—and I was surprised by my presumption. I never mentioned my imaginings to Larry, but soon after that visit (and four months after our initial blind date), he got down on bended knee and asked me to marry him.

"Gwen, I love you dearly. Will you marry me?" he asked tearfully. "We haven't known each other very long, but I know that my decision won't change. You are the one person with whom I want to live the remaining years of my life."

I was stunned. Though I knew in my heart that we would marry, and even knew *where* we would marry, I hadn't expected a proposal so soon. I was terrified but decided to take the leap.

"Yes, of course I will. I love you very much too," I responded as we embraced.

Less than a year later, in the Queen of Angels chapel, we got married. With seven children between us and a multitude of grandchildren, we are a large family, and yet there was just enough room in the pews for our family and friends. My initial count was on target!

As we exchanged our vows, I thought about how our separate journeys of laughter and tears had brought us to this moment. I looked into Larry's loving eyes and realized I had no fear. I could trust him. I could let go. It was the dawn of a new life.

I announced my retirement almost a year before my actual departure from work. There were tasks I needed to complete, lengthy good-byes I needed to say, and a new life I needed to plan. Over the months that followed, my husband and I traveled in search of a home, one that would be our very own. We followed family and friends to communities throughout the Southwest and to both the East and West Coasts.

Then, unexpectedly, at a family gathering, an uncle suggested a very different venture: he recommended that we take a vacation to a small resort town called Branson in the Ozark Mountains of Missouri. We had never heard of this town, nor had we visited the state of Missouri, but the more we learned about the area, the more interested we became. "Good people," my uncle said, "with great country music to enjoy." We pulled out a map, found the town, and planned a trip.

When we flew in to the Branson airport, we quickly realized we were embarking on a journey of a different nature. The lobby of the airport is designed to look like a log cabin. Its rustic general store, its restaurant known for barbecue ribs, and wooden benches and rocking chairs situated throughout give visitors a sense of having arrived in the country. We were surprised as much as we were charmed.

We rented a timeshare for the week, and after we settled in and sorted through the many pamphlets on activities in the area, we decided to go to Mel's Hard Luck Diner for a quick bite to eat. We knew nothing about the restaurant before we arrived, except that a friend asked us to say hello to the proprietor, as he had once been her supervisor at another location. As we sat down, we were surprised to learn that the music was live. Very live.

All the waiters and waitresses at the café are professional vocalists, and they take turns singing as they serve. They each have a specialty—gospel, opera, Broadway, country. Our waitress sang old gospel songs, and her passion brought me to tears. I couldn't believe I was so emotional, but in this restaurant, while eating my grilled-chicken salad, I cried.

During our stay, we went to a few performances, one of which was an outdoor production of *The Shepherd of the Hills*. Neither of us knew anything about the story behind the play, so we were a little lost by the narrative. We watched as horses and sheep crossed the dirt stage, saw a cabin burn down and men with rifles shoot at each other. We got the gist but little more. Sitting next to me, however, was a beautiful Mennonite woman, radiant in the setting sun, and she caught my attention even more than the drama itself.

"Is this the first time you've seen the play?" she asked at intermission, noticing me trying to read the program in the dimming light.

"Yes, we are visitors. The concierge suggested we go see this production," I replied.

"I've been coming for years," she said with a smile. "These are my nieces," she continued, pointing to two adolescents sitting to her right. "I've accompanied them from Kansas. All of us in our community have read the book *The Shepherd of the Hills*. I think you would like it too, and it would help you understand the play."

"Thank you. I'll try to read the book. You're from Kansas? Do you have a lot of tornadoes?" I asked, thinking of stories about Tornado Alley.

"Oh, we've had a few," she replied, smiling sweetly at my question.

"Has one ever hit your home?" I persisted, thinking about the what-ifs of moving to this part of the country.

"One did, but we simply rebuilt the house. After all, a house is just a house." She grinned.

I was flabbergasted; she was not attached to her home or her belongings. Was that why she seemed so free?

"The square dance is starting," she said. "This is for the entire audience. Don't you want to go down?" Actually, I wanted to talk with her, but in the end Larry and I joined the dancing crowd onstage.

Throughout the remainder of the play, I thought about the peacefulness of the woman next to me, I thought about my attachment to "things," and I wondered what it would be like to live in this part of the country.

A few days later, we decided to visit the quaint village of Eureka Springs in Arkansas—about an hour's drive from our timeshare. Walking up and down the town's hilly streets and into stores selling the wares of local artists, I found my pace slowing and my heart opening. Just outside one of the shops, a guitarist sang Randy Travis's "Forever and Ever, Amen," and I thought of my dad. He spent several of his childhood years not far from this small town, and Randy Travis was one of his favorite singers. As my eyes welled with tears, I thought, *Am I coming home?*

Over the next year, Larry and I traveled back to the region three more times. We looked for homes and explored the surrounding territory. Wherever we wandered during our stays, we were asked if we had read *The Shepherd of the Hills*, by Harold Bell Wright. We had not, but finding the book was easy. Most stores and hotels prominently displayed copies of the 1907 best seller. The story, written in the dialect of the times, unfolds in the Ozark Mountains of southern Missouri. It draws the reader into the lives of the local mountain people and focuses on deep family sorrows to which all can relate. At the heart of the narrative is the love of two fathers for a deceased child, two fathers who eventually make a decision to either forgive the other or lash out in revenge. The choice that each parent makes shapes not only what unfolds in the story but also what evolves in the mountain community we were visiting. Reading the book both provided me with a greater appreciation for the history of this community and helped me to realize why we were drawn to the area. We needed to *pause*—that we might see, hear, and understand.

> *Here and there among men, there are those who pause in the hurried rush to listen to the call of a life that is more real… He who sees and hears too much is cursed for a dreamer, a fanatic, or a fool, by the mad mob who, having eyes, see not, ears and hear not, and refuse to understand…*
>
> *Pete knew a world unseen by us, and we, therefore, fancied ourselves wiser than he. The wind in the pines, the rustle of the leaves, the murmur of the brook, the growl of thunder, and the voices of the night were all understood and answered by him. The flowers, the trees, the rocks, the hills, the clouds were to him, not lifeless things, but living friends, who laughed and wept with him as he was gay or sorrowful. "Poor Pete," we said. Was he in truth, poorer or richer than we?*

The character Pete was indeed "richer than we," and about a year after our first visit, we decided to pack our belongings and move into the Ozark Mountains. When we finally made our decision, our friends and family were astonished. They could not understand why anyone from sunny California would willingly choose to move to the backwoods of southern Missouri. Our reasons for the decision were multiple and did not include the weather.

In this small but vibrant town, we felt comfortable, joyful, and excited—and we were in awe of the natural beauty surrounding us: Table Rock Lake, with more than eight hundred miles of shoreline; the dense forests of the Ozark Mountains; the plentitude of wildlife. It was and is a wonderland of sorts, where we could go to a live performance or walk in the woods or go out on the lake. But there was a deeper reason behind our choice as well. In this locale, I felt closer to my heart. Admittedly, there was no logic to why I felt this way; it simply was—and is—the case. The kindness and generosity of the people, their openness and honesty, and their Heartland values brought me home to myself. Perhaps because of this homecoming, one day something extraordinary occurred.

On a crisp Sunday morning, we walked into church and found seats toward the back. I knelt down to pray, as I always do, and in the silence of my heart I repeated a paraphrase of an ancient prayer: *Dear Lord, grant that I might see you more clearly, love you more dearly, follow you more nearly, in all that I do today.* As I looked up to sit back in the pew, I was so bewildered by what I saw that I could not move—I simply stared in disbelief.

Scanning the church to the right and to the left, I saw angels in every direction, helping people. They were luminous, in long white robes. Some accompanied folks to their seats, some sat with small children, some walked with the disabled down the aisle, some gazed at babies in their mothers' arms. Each angel was lovingly present to one person in particular. As I watched in awe, utterly dumbfounded by what I was seeing, the angels turned in unison and looked directly at me. In that moment, I thought, *Am I going to die?*

The angels seemed quite aware that I could see them, and I somehow knew that I was supposed to see them, but I did not know why. We simply looked at one another, without speaking a word, and then they faded mysteriously from sight.

Throughout the Mass, I searched for the angels, thinking that I might see them again, but I did not. I wondered if I had imagined what I had seen, but I knew that to be unlikely because I couldn't have conceived of such a scenario. In the end, I accepted that somehow I was given a glimpse of another reality, a world of celestial care that is usually not visible—at least not to me.

On Christmas Eve, we were again at church, when another angelic encounter occurred. Just before Mass, the musician began to play his guitar and sing. I couldn't see him, but his voice carried throughout the church, captivating all of us. Within the first few notes, many fought back tears. His passion transported us into our own hearts' desire.

Then I *felt* the angels; it was as though the heavens opened up and the angels filled the sanctuary. The space was crowded with them, and it was overwhelming. Finally, I saw the musician, Tony Melendez. No arms, playing the guitar with his toes, singing from the fathomlessness of his heart. No wonder the angels came. One note can reach the universe if it is sung from such pure depths. When the Mass was over, not one person left his or her seat. All waited for Tony to exit. Collectively, we had experienced the miraculous.

Why now? Why here? I wondered. Was this place really that different from any other area? Its natural splendor is undeniable, but sand dunes are incredible to behold, beaches can be dazzling, and even the wilds of the inner city have their own beauty. So why these blessed encounters?

One day I went to a crafts fair in the historic downtown area of Branson. As I wandered from booth to booth, looking at woodwork, paintings, stitchery, and jewelry, I noticed an artisan throwing clay on a pottery wheel. When he saw me looking at his ceramic bowls, he introduced himself and then asked, "Where are you from?" His question was one I had been asked many times since I had moved to the area. Branson is a tourist site, and most of its occupants are visitors.

"Originally from California, but we live here now," I responded.

"That's great!" he said, smiling. "I moved to Branson eleven years ago from Ventura, and I've never regretted it. So tell me, have you gotten involved yet?"

"We're just settling in," I explained. "Most of the boxes are unpacked now, so we'll soon be free to participate more."

"Well, when you're ready, you'll find there is something for everyone to do. We all volunteer," he offered. "Maybe you'd like to help at the hospital, or perhaps you'd like to tutor children after school. What's your interest?"

I shared my past experiences of working with Habitat for Humanity and several different inner-city soup kitchens. I told him about my training in counseling and in education. And I thought, *What an unexpected conversation.* The potter was smiling; he could see my excitement. Then he added, "We take care of each other here. We're like a big family. You'll see."

We take care of each other? Could this be the reason for the miraculous?

When we returned to California in 2013 to spend time with our loved ones, I visited a Jewish friend who is an energy worker in Laguna Beach. She began the session with a short prayer and then explained how she would proceed. As I sat in her room of ancient symbols and fresh-picked flowers, I watched as a single butterfly fluttered through the open door and danced about the space. I was entranced.

About midway through the healing session, my friend hesitated and said, "I need to tell you this, Gwen. There is a very, *very* large angel standing behind you. Are you aware of this?" she asked.

"I'm aware of Presence, of someone very loving near me," I replied.

"Its wings wrap around you and cross at your heart, Gwen. It is very big, very muscular. The angel wants you to know that it is always with you. Does this make *any* sense?" she inquired.

"Yes, it does. I usually can feel the angel, but even if I don't, I know it is with me."

At different times during the hour-long session, my friend would again pause, smile, and mention once more the "very large" angel; she was enchanted by, and felt grateful to see, what I could only sense in that moment.

Letting Go into Perfect Love

My grandmother Mamo, who rescued me each year of my childhood during summer harvest by taking me to San Diego, lived well into her nineties. When I could, I visited her at the retirement complex where she lived.

"Why doesn't God take me home, Gwen?" she would ask pleadingly as she sat in her lift chair.

"Your grandpa is in heaven," she continued. "Why doesn't God take me too?"

"Maybe God wants you here for us," I suggested. "And the people you meet in the dining room, the ones you talk with every day, maybe they need you too." I was not entirely certain how to respond to her question.

"Maybe so, Gwen, maybe so. I do talk to them about God," she said, sighing softly, her voice trailing off. "But I long to be with your grandpa, Gwen. He treated me so well. What good am I now? There's nothing more I can do."

In her heyday, Mamo was a phenomenal baker. She was accustomed to making cakes from scratch, her buttery pound cake actually prepared from a pound of this and a pound of that. Her pies were similarly recipe-perfect, with crusts done just so. She shared these masterpieces with family and friends, churches, and her bridge group. She even baked mini-pies for trick-or-treaters on Halloween. No one could come close to replicating the quality of her sweet delights. Baking was an art form for Mamo, and a boxed mix of anything was an unacceptable counterfeit. We would not dare to make a pecan pie or peach cobbler if she was visiting, as our efforts would surely have been disappointing.

Mamo was also a talented landscape painter, though at times she strayed from the desert and mountain scenes she loved to capture the beauty of local flowers.

"Would you like this painting?" she asked one day, pointing to a still life of roses hanging above her walker. She had finished it years earlier, when her eyesight was clear, her hands nimble.

"I'd love it, Mamo," I said. "I will put it in my living room."

"That makes me happy, Gwen. Remember me when you look at it, okay?" she said.

"I'll always remember you, Mamo. You helped me so much when I was a child, and I am forever grateful."

Months later, when she passed away, no one was surprised. She had waited a long time to be reunited with her spouse, and we were happy for her. But her demise left certain matters unfinished; questions about her estate arose, and old sorrows between her stepchildren and her birth children were resurrected.

Just as I climbed into bed one night, settling under my comforter, I suddenly heard Mamo's voice.

It wasn't supposed to be this way, she clearly said. *It wasn't supposed to be this way.*

I quickly sat up in bed, startled by what I had heard. I could sense her visage; she was looking at me imploringly.

It wasn't supposed to be this way, she said again. *I didn't know I would live this long.*

In a flash, I understood that Mamo had imagined that she had divided her estate fairly among her children, but her long life and lengthy stay in the retirement home had depleted much of the money she had perhaps intended for part of the family, while her other relatives had inherited her land. In the end, her children were divided financially the same way they had been emotionally as youngsters—into those with and those without.

As I sat in my room, glimpsing this image of Mamo, I realized that she thought she had done the right thing. Her perfect cakes and perfect pies had mirrored the perfection she expected of herself. I saw how hard she had tried to meet her ideals. And in that moment, I realized that she needed my understanding.

When I wrote to my mother, and she to her siblings, about this encounter, I felt Mamo's presence again. This time she was at peace; she felt understood.

Her painting, with its three red roses stretching upward and a single bud reaching yet higher, hangs quietly in my home, a memorial to the hopes and dreams of an Arkansas woman who divorced her wandering husband in the late 1920s and trekked across the country with her baby daughter to clean homes in the California desert, where she met her true love nearly a decade later. When I look at this painting, I think of Mamo and women everywhere who have struggled with adversity and triumphed. I imagine my father's mother giving birth to twins alone alongside the fields of Oklahoma, I think of my own mother losing two of her nine children and nearly her life, and I remember the country quilters who shared their stories as they methodically stitched one scrap of fabric to another. When I look at this painting, I think of the generations before me and those that will follow.

We are journeymen, you and I, and the master craftsman is life. We learn quickly sometimes, but more commonly we learn very slowly, and we travel far and near to grasp our trade. We all get sidetracked at times in our quest for meaning and perfection, but one way or another, through the assistance of kind strangers, the patience of therapists or healers or friends, and the prodding of those who may seem to be foes, we are brought back home to ourselves.

My former spiritual director, Sister Grace, reminded me several times over the span of the years when she counseled me that we are born to become Love.

"Every challenge helps guide us, Gwen," she explained patiently. "Our families, our friends, even our enemies help us in ways we don't expect."

"What do you mean, our enemies help us?" I protested.

"They are the best teachers!" she exclaimed. "They couldn't be more ideal. Who else will stomp on your dreams and force you to see differently?" she said, smiling wryly.

"I suppose so," I responded doubtfully. "At least they can help us see the choice before us."

"Exactly!" she acknowledged excitedly. "Because of their offensive ways, you get to choose whether or not to love yourself. They show you the dividing line between disrespect and self-respect."

Mamo faced just such a divide when she was a very young woman who made the decision to leave her unfaithful spouse. Holding tight to her toddler, she got on a bus on the outskirts of Fayetteville, Arkansas, and headed for California, not knowing what awaited her. Like Mamo, we all travel with our crushed dreams through the underbrush of life, looking for our castle in the sky. Along the way, we meet and walk with friends and foes, family members, and our children. We may take a certain path only to discover that we have traveled that same trail several times before. We may even walk that well-trodden route a few more times before we choose another. We are creatures of habit, and often, unless we are roused by heartaches, we proceed routinely and sometimes blindly, doing the best we can. One day, my hairstylist tearfully shared such a story.

"I don't understand it," she began as she cut my wet hair. "I thought Juan was different from my former boyfriend. But now I see that he is just the same." Tears welled in her big brown eyes.

"I'm so sorry to hear this," I responded, wondering if she was going to be able to finish my hair.

"There's only one constant, Gwen, and it is me!" she exclaimed. "Somehow I attract this behavior; I just have to figure out how and why. I don't want to go through life like this."

As she talked about her situation, I pondered what I should say or not—she was decades younger than I was, with much more life to live.

"You're a wiser woman than I was at your age," I finally ventured. "I needed a counselor to help me with my situation. When I met with the counselor, I told her, 'I never want to repeat this again. Whatever I need to learn, please help me learn it.'"

"And did she help you?" my stylist asked.

"Yes. It took time, but the process really helped me," I replied. "Mostly I discovered who I was and am, and I learned to value myself."

"Well, I need to do something," she said, looking into the mirror at me. "I don't want to waste my best years."

"I don't think we *waste* our years," I said reassuringly. "Sometimes it just takes us a while to figure out what our next step might be."

Over the deafening hum of the hair dryer, the clamor of ringing phones, and the loud conversations of other stylists with their clients, my hairdresser friend talked more about her situation. And while she did, I thought of how we are all so much alike.

Some among us seem to be more equipped for life's journey than we may feel we are. From a distance, their lives appear to be ideal— their laughter erupts easily; contagious love fills their homes. While they manage the daily challenges of life seemingly effortlessly, we may tromp through the thorny thickets of human sorrows with bloodied knees, aching backs, and burdened hearts. Doubt and fear may cloud our vision, while our comrades may seem energized by possibilities. We share the same destination, but our life rewards and hardships differ.

Who among us does not look at our carefree neighbor and think, *This is not fair*? But in reality, is the question itself "fair"?

Years back, I took several classes in spirituality as part of my degree in theology. One of these classes focused on the stages of spiritual development. To illustrate these developmental junctures, the professor presented us with a panel of four women. One was in her twenties, another in her forties, another in her fifties, and the last one in her seventies. The professor asked each panel member the same questions and asked us to compare their responses to the questions. His hope was that we would better understand the concrete differences between the stages of life by listening to these women.

I remember little of the first two women, because their answers were too familiar to me. They worried about whether they prayed sufficiently, whether they crafted their prayers efficaciously, whether they understood this or that. In general, they tried to do everything right and worried about whether they were successful at what they were doing.

It was the last woman—the one in her seventies—who captured my attention. She was not worried about anything. Her lightheartedness was entrancing, and I thought, *I want to be like her.* She was not concerned about whether she prayed correctly or not; for her, prayer was a conversation with an indwelling God of love. She was not anxious about the challenges of the day, "Everything will work out," she said, smiling. I was mesmerized by her freedom, her confidence, and her radiance. And I wondered, *Will I have to wait another four decades before I know her peace?*

At the time, Johnny was a baby, and his bubbly nature made him everyone's sweetheart. He was the child who was passed from one stranger to another, as each offered coos and giggles. He was a cuddly bear of sorts—but so was the woman in her seventies. Both were unabashedly loving, accepting, and joyful. Who would have thought that a baby and a seventy-year-old could be so much alike?

It is only in retrospect that I have come to see how the journey we travel is circular. Life's summit is elusive because the terminus is also the starting point. Ultimately, any life path we choose brings us full circle. When we meet ourselves again, our horizons may have shifted, our joys may have expanded, and our hearts may have softened. And then we begin again. We travel until we *become* Love, as Sister Grace explained.

T. S. Eliot, in his last verses of the poem "Little Gidding," wrote:

We shall not cease from exploration
And the end of all our exploring
Will be to arrive where we started
And know the place for the first time.
Through the unknown, remembered gate
When the last of earth left to discover
Is that which was the beginning...

Photos of my children are clustered in several areas of my home—photos of them as adults, and photos of them when they were quite young. When I look at the first set of pictures, I think about what my adult children are doing, I think about their relationships, I think about the complexities of their lives, and I feel very proud of them. I know they are doing the best they can.

The images of my children in their toddler years evoke something very different. When I look at these, I am brought back to heart memories: I remember when I first held them, covered in vernix and pink with struggle; I remember their first cry and the fear I felt when Johnny arrived lifeless and without a sound; I remember their tiny fingers and how they held on to mine; and I remember being entranced as I looked down into their swollen little eyes. As my heart filled with love, my fear faded away—there was simply no place for it.

When I see the photos of my little ones who are now adults, I feel protective as I relive those early years. From this heart place, I am again brought back to my original intention of wanting only the best for my children. I look deep into the face of the child caught in the photograph and know what awaits him or her. Time becomes fluid, floating between decades; the present melds with the past, and a collage of stories emerges. I see my child, I see the adult he or she has become, and I see myself.

I tried to shelter my children from unhappiness, but life had different plans for them. I realize now that tragedy spares no one; it just courts each of us differently. One way or another, it finds a path into our hearts, and there we do battle with the intruder. Armed with childhood imaginings and with trust in tomorrow's benevolences, we crusade for truth, for meaning, for love—not knowing that sorrow is often the gateway to that which we seek.

When it is time, we walk the corridors of our heart, retrieving the shattered threads of once-believed dreams. Perhaps, long after tears have dried and hope has faded, we find what was always there but not seen—and then our desolation gives rise to a new spring.

My dad loved to travel, but with seven children, even the largest station wagon was insufficient. His solution was to convert an old bus into a motor home by replacing the seats on one side with bunk beds and removing half of the remaining seats for a makeshift kitchenette. We'd climb into our blue-painted bus, argue about who got to sleep on the top bunk, and ride for hours.

One of our trips took us to the Grand Canyon. We arrived on a cold December morning, after spending the night on the road. Snow covered the walkways and blanketed the canyon's rocky gorge. Our Southern California clothing was no match for the winter winds. My bare legs were red with frost, my toes cold through my thin sneakers. When my brothers sent snowballs flying, we girls erupted in delight and scurried back to the shelter of the bus, where we spent most of our time. The canyon's expansiveness was more than I could grasp; I was both scared and inspired. Mostly, though, I was cold.

About fifteen years later, Ron and I spent the night at the canyon while en route to California to visit my family for Christmas. Leaving Indiana in the very early morning, we took turns driving, stopping only for gas and quick refreshments. About twenty-four hours later, we arrived and quickly collapsed onto our bed. Little Matt awakened me in the morning with his usual giggles and smiles. Holding him in my arms, I opened the curtain to see the snow-covered canyon. Unlike before, as I stared into the distance, I felt an eerie silence.

Fast-forward twenty years: I took my younger three children on a marathon trip through the Southwest. We flew into Albuquerque and traveled across New Mexico and into Arizona, visiting one site after another, experiencing white-water rafting, hiking, and jeep trips. Eventually we reached the canyon. The sun was high and warm, and the children ran down the paths. I can still hear their laughter and feel their delight. The expansiveness that had once seemed overwhelming was now intoxicating.

More recently, Larry and I visited the Grand Canyon once again. We spent Christmas in Sedona and went on a tour to the canyon's rim. The roads were icy, and snow was piled high on either side of the road. As our van forged its way, we were grateful we hadn't driven ourselves. "Everyone out," the driver announced, "and remember to be back in the van at four thirty sharp!"

We slowly climbed out of the van and walked only a few feet before I slipped on the ice. As I sat on the snow, I erupted in giggles. Then, hand in hand, Larry and I tried again to walk to the rim, and together we landed on our bottoms. This time we both laughed heartily. "Guess we're getting old," my husband said.

When we finally reached the canyon's rim, I was spellbound by the majesty, the beauty, and the vastness of the canyon, and warmed by the lightheartedness of our adventure.

Four separate trips to the Grand Canyon, each of which left me with very different impressions. What was the variable? What changed? Certainly, the canyon itself did not—it has remained the same for centuries. The only variable was perspective, fashioned by time and circumstance.

Upon the arrival of each of my youngest two sons, a gentle custodian who cleaned the office building in which I worked gave me a shiny silver dollar. "This is for your baby," he said. "It's not much, of course, but I hope it travels with him through life. Sometimes 'In God We Trust' is all we can hold on to, but that is all that we really need." Thirty years later, his gift is the only one that remains.

Our torments eventually bring us to a place of trust—in the divine, in the universe, in the unnamed One, in Life. This trust is not the naive notion that we will be spared hardships and disappointments. Rather, it is the hard-earned trust that comes from glimpsing the consecrated journey for which we were created.

Most of us have photos of ourselves as happy babies, much like the one of my toddler self smiling with my new dolly in front of the Christmas tree. As infants, we didn't *think* about love; we simply knew it. Then, as we began to walk life's craggy terrain, our knowing of love slipped into the shadows of our experience…and fear emerged.

Much of our life journey is about searching for this early love, this Perfect Love. More often than not, our most effective guides are those that figuratively and literally push us up against the wall. Health crises and sometimes devastating circumstances provide us with opportunity after opportunity to address our fear through the choices before us—freedom or enslavement, self-value or self-depreciation, love or hate, trust or despair.

Our unlikely and unwanted teachers goad us to make decisions that ultimately help us rediscover the love that has always awaited us. This love is not the transient love nurtured with flowers and layered in sweet dreams. It is the phoenix love that arises from the ashes of our struggles to free our hearts and give us glee. This powerful love overshadows storybook fantasies and late-night reveries. It casts out all fear and walks with us through the maze of our misperceptions to a place of compassion and reconciliation. Though it may take a lifetime, we relearn what it means to bask in the love we knew when we were just toddlers.

When I hiked barefoot on the hot desert sands of my youth, I thought I was alone, but I was not. When I was immobilized by fear in my early years and knew not what to do, I thought I was alone, but I was not. When I hung from the cliff's rocky crest on Salt Spring Island, there was not a person anywhere within calling distance, but I was not alone. Through the forested trails of my Connecticut retreat; during the long, haunting nights of the California Hoffman process; on my walks in the beautiful Ozark hills among butterflies, deer, and armadillo, I was not—and still am not—alone.

We are never alone, no matter where we might be or what challenge may besiege us. As we travel the back roads of our life, learning to become Love, we are accompanied by the seen and the unseen. I now know with certainty that angels go with us. At times we are privileged to see them or feel them. Other times we are left with whispers or prods that lead us to do something that helps us or someone else. Because of the whispers of an angel, I was suddenly aware that three-year-old Matt was in danger, only to find him standing on a high windowsill, preparing to jump. Through the nudges of an angel, I knew that Andrew was hurt and even knew the culprit causing his suffering. Because of my strong and repeated inner urgings from an angel to call home, warning me that something was terribly wrong, I discovered that Sarah was having a severe episode. In each of these situations and so many more, angels prompted me to take action that ultimately helped my children and me.

The unexplained can be interpreted as purposeful or accidental.

But as I unravel the details of the various circumstances in my life and look honestly at the consequences, I am left with only one conclusion: all of life has meaning, and through our tragedies and disappointments, as well as our joys, we are lovingly guided to more profound realizations of that meaning.

Deep within each of us, there is a well of love—a place of wholeness, a place of completeness. This sacred well is alive with wisdom and tenderness. It is our true self; it is where Perfect Love resides. This all-encompassing and unconditional love draws each of us home. And ever so slowly, as we grow more confident in our journey, letting go into Perfect Love becomes a way of being.

Acknowledgments

For patiently understanding my long hours at the computer and for encouraging me to write, I'd like to thank my husband, Larry. His unwavering support kept my heart open and my hopes alive. I am also deeply grateful to my children, who unknowingly accompanied me through this process in memories long past and in dreams yet to come.

I am forever indebted to my two spiritual directors, Sister Grace Myerjack, MM, and Father Simon Harak, SJ. Their patient and always-loving guidance helped me experience the bliss in life and know the love of God. I also thank the many counselors and healing professionals who caringly guided me to wholeness. In particular, I am grateful to Clare Goodwin, June Sinclair, and Jacqueline Lapa Sussman.

Finally, I am profoundly appreciative of the coaching and editing efforts of Annie Tucker Morgan. Her brilliance, wisdom, and amazing confidence helped me learn how to write, and by doing so, she opened a door to my soul.

About the Author

Gwendolyn M Plano spent most of her professional life in higher education. She taught and served as an administrator in colleges in New York, Connecticut, and California. She earned a Bachelor's Degree in nutrition from San Diego State University, was awarded a Master's Degree in Theology from the University of the State of New York and then completed a Master's Degree in Counseling from Iona College. Finally, Gwendolyn earned a Doctorate in Education from Columbia University. She is also a Reiki Master and a Certified LifeLine Practitioner.

SELECTED TITLES FROM SHE WRITES PRESS

*She Writes Press is an independent publishing company
founded to serve women writers everywhere.
Visit us at www.shewritespress.com.*

Loveyoubye: Hanging On, Letting Go, And Then There's The Dog
by Rossandra White $16.95, 978-1-938314-50-6
A soul-searching memoir detailing the painful, but ultimately liberating, disintegration of a twenty-five-year marriage.

Breathe: A Memoir of Motherhood, Death, and Family Conflict
by Kelly Kittel $16.95, 978-1-938314-78-0
A mother's heartbreaking account of losing two sons in the span of nine months—and learning, despite all the obstacles in her way, to find joy in life again.

Seeing Red: A Woman's Quest for Truth, Power, and the Sacred
by Lone Morch $16.95, 978-1-938314-12-4
One woman's journey over inner and outer mountains—a quest that takes her to the holy Mt. Kailas in Tibet, through a seven-year marriage, and into the arms of the fierce goddess Kali, where she discovers her powerful, feminine self.

Splitting the Difference: A Heart-Shaped Memoir by Tré Miller-Rodríguez
$19.95, 978-1-938314-20-9
When 34-year-old Tré Miller-Rodríguez's husband dies suddenly from a heart attack, her grief sends her on an unexpected journey that culminates in a reunion with the biological daughter she gave up at 18.

Don't Call Me Mother: A Daughter's Journey from Abandonment to Forgiveness by Linda Joy Myers $16.95, 978-1-938314-02-5
Linda Joy Myers's story of how she transcended the prisons of her childhood by seeking—and offering—forgiveness for her family's sins.

Think Better. Live Better. 5 Steps to Your Best Life by Francine Huss
$16.95, 978-1-938314-66-7
With the help of this guide, readers will learn to cultivate more creative thoughts, realign their mindset, and gain a new perspective on life.

CPSIA information can be obtained at www.ICGtesting.com
Printed in the USA
BVOW05s1331130514

353083BV00003B/9/P